Language in Education:
Theory and Practice

D1413108

ESL
THROUGH CONTENT-AREA
INSTRUCTION:
MATHEMATICS, SCIENCE,
SOCIAL STUDIES

ESL THROUGH CONTENT-AREA INSTRUCTION

MATHEMATICS
Theresa Corasaniti Dale
Gilberto J. Cuevas

SCIENCE
Carolyn Kessler
Mary Ellen Quinn

SOCIAL STUDIES
Melissa King
Barbara Fagan
Terry Bratt
Rod Baer

JoAnn Crandall, Editor

A publication of Center for Applied Linguistics

Prepared by Clearinghouse on Languages and Linguistics

PRENTICE HALL REGENTS Englewood Cliffs, New Jersey 07632

Library of Congress Cataloging-in-Publication Data

ESL through content-area instruction.

  Bibliography
  1. English language--Study and teaching--Foreign
speakers. I. Crandall, Jo Ann. II. Dale, Theresa
Corasaniti.
PE1128.A2E745 1987   428'.007   87-11563
ISBN 0-13-284373-0

LANGUAGE IN EDUCATION: Theory and Practice 67

Office of Educational
Research and Improvement
U.S. Department of Education

This publication was prepared with funding from the Office
of Educational Research and Improvement, U.S. Department of Education, under contract no. 400-82-009. The
opinions expressed in this report do not necessarily reflect
the positions or policies of OERI or ED.

Production Supervision by Martha Masterson
Cover design by Karen Stephens
Manufacturing Buyer: Lorraine Fumoso

Published 1987 by Prentice Hall, Inc.
A division of Simon & Schuster
Englewood Cliffs, NJ 07632

Printed in the United States of America

10 9 8 7 6 5 4 3 2 1

ISBN 0-13-284373-0 01

Prentice-Hall International (UK) Limited, London
Prentice-Hall of Australia Pty. Limited, Sydney
Prentice-Hall Canada Inc., Toronto
Prentice-Hall Hispanoamericana, S.A., Mexico
Prentice-Hall of India Private Limited, New Delhi
Prentice-Hall of Japan, Inc., Tokyo
Prentice-Hall of Southeast Asia Pte. Ltd., Singapore
Editora Prentice-Hall do Brasil, Ltda., Rio de Janeiro

Language in Education: Theory and Practice

ERIC (Educational Resources Information Center) is a nationwide network of information centers, each responsible for a given educational level or field of study. ERIC is supported by the Office of Educational Research and Improvement of the U.S. Department of Education. The basic objective of ERIC is to make current developments in educational research, instruction, and personnel preparation readily accessible to educators and members of related professions.

ERIC/CLL. The ERIC Clearinghouse on Languages and Linguistics (ERIC/CLL), one of the specialized clearinghouses in the ERIC system, is operated by the Center for Applied Linguistics (CAL). ERIC/CLL is specifically responsible for the collection and dissemination of information on research and application in languages and linguistics and its application to language teaching and learning.

LANGUAGE IN EDUCATION: THEORY AND PRACTICE. In addition to processing information, ERIC/CLL is also involved in information synthesis and analysis. The Clearinghouse commissions recognized authorities in languages and linguistics to write analyses of the current issues in their areas of specialty. The resultant documents, intended for use by educators and researchers, are published under the series title, Language in Education: Theory and Practice. The series includes practical guides for classroom teachers and extensive state-of-the-art papers.

This publication may be purchased directly from Prentice-Hall, Inc., Book Distribution Center, Route 59 at Brook Hill Dr., West Nyack, NY 10995, telephone (201) 767-5049. It also will be announced in the ERIC monthly abstract journal *Resources in Education (RIE)* and will be available from the ERIC Document Reproduction Service, Computer Microfilm International Corp., 3900 Wheeler Ave., Alexandria, VA 22304. See *RIE* for ordering information and ED number.

For further information on the ERIC system, ERIC/CLL, and CAL/Clearinghouse publications, write to ERIC Clearinghouse on Languages and Linguistics, Center for Applied Linguistics, 1118 22nd St. NW, Washington, DC 20037.

Gina Doggett, Editor, Language in Education

Contents

Content-Based ESL: An Introduction

The concept of integrating language instruction with subject matter instruction is not new to language educators. It has been attempted for many years in adult education, in university programs for foreign students, and in specialized language courses for scientists, businessmen, and other professionals. To some degree, it has also been a part of elementary and secondary school ESL programs, although actual content-based ESL courses are relatively new. This collection of essays—by classroom teachers, researchers, and teacher educators—describes some of the ways in which English language instruction is being integrated with science, mathematics, and social sciences in elementary, secondary, and college classes, and reviews some of the theoretical support for this approach.

Writing Across the Curriculum

The Bullock Report (1975) on English across the curriculum was the first overt expression of a growing movement away from the rhetorical, product-oriented writing class—divorced from other subject-matter classes—toward an approach that views writing as an integral part of any course within the curriculum. Although limited attention has long been given to business or technical writing at the secondary or adult/

tertiary level, attention to writing is appropriate in all content courses as a valuable means of learning (just as talking represents a way of learning). Although the language arts or writing teacher has been accorded a special role in helping students to find their own voice and to give form to their thoughts and feelings, teachers of mathematics, science, social studies, and other subjects also have a responsibility to see that writing skills are applied to authentic tasks such as lab reports, explanations of principles and theorems, discussions of historical causes and effects, or comparisons of religious or cultural institutions. Tchudi and Tchudi (1983) list the following benefits of teaching writing in the content areas:

1. Writing about a subject helps students learn.

2. Writing about content has a practical payoff. (Students write better when they spend more time writing.)

3. Content writing often motivates reluctant writers.

4. Content writing develops all language skills.

5. Teaching writing teaches thinking.

Reading in the Content Areas

A similar trend has developed in the field of reading: Language arts and reading specialists urge that reading be "taught" in all content areas, while they, in turn, introduce texts in their reading classes that are relevant to and representative of those that students will read in their content-area classes. This change has required reading teachers to teach more than literature; and mathematics, science, and other subject-matter teachers to teach more than their subject matter. Since reading is a way of acquiring information and learning, it is a skill to be addressed in all classes. The purposes for reading, the types of texts presented, and the kinds or reading skills required differ by discipline and task; students need to acquire a variety of skills that they can apply to their reading assignments, whether reading for information, for pleasure, or for guidance in performing a task. Content-area teachers must recognize that they, too, are "reading" teachers; likewise, reading or language arts or English teachers must understand that their "content" may go beyond literature.

A great deal of research has been published on the types of texts and the kinds of skills and strategies involved in reading in the content areas, as well as descriptions of program models and curricula that integrate reading with content areas (Dupuis, 1984; Herber, 1978; Vacca, 1981). Dupuis (1984) found that "Over twenty textbooks are currently published to teach teachers how to deal with reading in content classrooms" (p. 2), although some subject-matter areas such as mathematics, science, and social studies have received more attention than other areas, such as music, health, or physical education.

Content in Language Instruction

While reading and writing theorists and practitioners have been concerned with using reading and writing to learn (not just helping students to learn to read and write), a similar trend has been evident in language instruction, where the focus is not just on learning the language, but in using it as a medium to learn something else. Although traditional language teaching has focused on grammar or literature, and more recently, on communicative competence or language use in a largely oral and interpersonal sense, a number of different segments of the language teaching profession have recognized the importance of focusing on content as well as language.

In English-for-specific-purposes (ESP) curricula, the goal of language instruction is to provide access to texts, seminars, lectures, and, broadly, the entire disciplines of such fields as engineering, science or technology, business or economics, medicine, law, or other professions. In teaching the particular vocabulary, discourse styles, and syntax of science texts, written or oral, the ESP course uses materials and activities drawn from the field, focusing on the ways in which the language is used to convey or represent particular thoughts or ideas. Within adult ESL programs, the focus often shifts to skilled or semiskilled jobs, with special-purpose English courses designed to assist adults in becoming welders, electronic assemblers, technicians, clerical workers, and the like. In both adult ESL and ESP, the integration of language and content is accomplished through coordinated efforts of teachers in both fields and the language teacher's use of texts (sometimes simplified or adapted) and activities drawn from the field of study.

Foreign language (FL) instruction has also focused on academic content in delivering FL immersion programs in which children receive all or part of their education *through* the medium of another language, thus acquiring the language simultaneously with learning the academic content of mathematics, or science, or whatever portion of the curriculum is taught through the language. The desire to develop optimal ways to present this content so as to keep it understandable to the student who is only beginning to learn the language of instruction parallels the concerns of content-based ESL teachers.

Within the field of ESL, models abound for combining language and content instruction. One of these, ESP, was discussed previously. Another model teams ESL teachers in an "adjunct" relationship with academic subject-matter teachers in a particular field. Public schools offer "sheltered immersion" programs, in which the subject-matter teacher uses the insights of the FL immersion class and the content-based ESL or specific-purpose ESL class to provide understandable content in English-medium instruction to students with limited English. In both FL immersion and sheltered-immersion programs, according to Curtain (1986):

1. There is a focus on meaning rather than on form. There is no overt error correction.

2. Linguistic modifications such as simplified

speech and controlled vocabulary that are necessary for comprehensible input are used.

3. Instructional language has contextual clues to help convey meaning.

4. Conversational interaction—usually the subject content—is interesting and real to the students.

5. Languages of instruction are kept very carefully separated.

6. Students are allowed a silent period and do not have to speak until they are ready.

Why Content-Based Instruction?

The bases for the increasing interest in content-based language instruction are varied. Developments in second language acquisition theory and insights from practice within the various fields of language instruction have both fueled the interest.

Within second language acquisition theory, perhaps the most important influence has been an emerging emphasis on the role that meaningful, understandable input plays in the acquisition of another language. Krashen (1981, 1982) has drawn parallels between first and second language acquisition and has suggested that the kinds of input that children get from their caretakers ("caretaker speech") should serve as a model for teachers in the input they provide to second language learners, regardless of age. Input must be comprehensible to the learner (at or just above the learner's level) and be offered in such a way as to allow multiple opportunities to understand and use the language. Krashen's "Monitor Model" suggests that if comprehensible input is provided and the student or acquirer does not feel a great deal of anxiety, then acquisition will take place.

One way of reducing the anxiety and also increasing the potential relevance and meaningfulness of the experience is to provide interesting texts and activities.

Krashen has recently emphasized the importance of extensive reading for pleasure as a means of language acquisition, as well as the role of writing. He recommends using texts and activities that are not grammar- or drill-based, but instead are interesting and authentic, dealing with real-world ideas, problems, and activities.

Krashen posits a dichotomy between acquisition and learning, with one (acquisition) serving to initiate all language and the other (learning) serving only as a monitor or editor, activated when the learner has time and is focusing on the correctness of his or her language. Thus, he stresses natural acquisition opportunities that are structured only enough to make them comprehensible to the acquirer.

In another dichotomy, Cummins (1979, 1981) has hypothesized two different kinds of language proficiency: basic interpersonal communication skills (BICS), which are language skills used in interpersonal relations or in informal situations whose extra-linguistic and linguistic context provide relatively easy access to meaning; and cognitive academic language proficiency (CALP), which is the kind of language proficiency required to make sense of and use academic language in less contextually rich (or more context-reduced) situations. Cummins suggests that BICS are relatively easy to acquire, taking only 1 to 2 years, but that CALP is much more difficult, taking from 5 to 7 years and necessitating direct teaching of the language in the academic context.

Given Cummins' hypothesis, it is somewhat easier to understand why students who have left ESL classes to enter mainstream classes (where English is the medium of instruction) often have difficulty and fall further and further behind in their academic work. Their seeming communicative competence and fluency is deceptive; although they can talk with their peers, engage in informal conversation with their teachers, read simple narratives, or write informal notes or letters, they are not able to deal with the more abstract, formal, contextually reduced language of the texts, tests, lectures, or discussions of science, or mathematics, or social studies.

Many content-based ESL programs have developed to provide students with an opportunity to learn CALP, as well as to provide a less abrupt transition from the ESL classroom to an all-English-medium academic program. Content-based ESL courses—whether taught by the ESL teacher, the content-area teacher, or some combination—provide direct instruction in the special language of the subject matter, while focusing attention as much or more on the subject matter itself.

This Collection

This combined focus—on the subject matter and the English that is used to communicate it—is the basis for this collection of essays. The authors of the three essays represent a broad range of experience as practitioners and researchers. They share a commitment to exploring the ways in which content and language instruction can be best integrated, and they are all relative pioneers in this endeavor.

The authors of "ESL and Science" are a teacher educator (Kessler) and a secondary school science teacher (Quinn). Together, they have undertaken a number of experimental or pilot science programs, developing curricula and activities to enable the limited-English-proficient (LEP) student to understand and take part in the science program and documenting the kinds of progress made.

Dale and Cuevas, the authors of "Integrating Mathematics and Language Teaching," have worked together on a number of mathematics projects for LEP children, with Cuevas bringing the mathematics insights and experience (as well as sensitivity to language issues in mathematics), and Dale bringing the linguistic insights and experience. Both have taught at a number of levels: Cuevas is a teacher educator and Dale has worked with both elementary school children and college freshmen and sophomores. Much of their work has involved the investigation of linguistic barriers to math problem-solving and to the development of materials and curricula to deal with them.

The authors of "ESL and Social Studies Instruction" are all ESL specialists and teachers who work together in one school system. They have developed one of the first secondary school ESL programs to address both the cultural and linguistic requirements for ESL students to function effectively in American social studies classes. Besides the practical experience of having to develop curricula and materials, several members of the team have also been involved in teacher education, providing another source of insight into the kinds of problems inherent in integrating language and content instruction.

These three essays provide an excellent introduction to the rationale for integrating language and content instruction, and offer concrete examples of ways in which this integration can be accomplished. Although the focus is on ESL, the insights can be applied to other languages as well and may lead the language teacher to consider the materials and activities of other fields as a kind of content—to be used alongside the focus on language structure and the culture(s) of people who speak the language—adaptable for use in the language classroom.

The use of content from other fields offers the language teacher an opportunity to enrich the language classroom. By providing a more interesting class, teachers motivate students to master the more abstract and difficult language that characterizes the various content areas. Communicative competence is more than appropriate informal use of the language, it also includes the ability to read, discuss, and write about complex and abstract ideas drawn from history, science, mathematics, or any educational field.

Integrating Language and Mathematics Learning

Theresa Corasaniti Dale
Center for Applied Linguistics

Gilberto J. Cuevas, Ph.D.
University of Miami

Picture a seventh- or eighth-grade classroom in which about half the students are nonnative English speakers with varying degrees of English proficiency. The teacher is about to present a mathematics lesson dealing with the properties of equality. She begins by writing the following on the blackboard:

$$(6+5) + 4 \;\square\; 6 + (5 + 4)$$

She points to the number sentence on each side of the empty square and asks the class: "Are they equal?" An English-proficient student answers: "Yes, they are." The discussion continues:

Teacher: *(pointing to a limited-English-proficient (LEP) student)* How do you know?

LEP Student: They equal.

Teacher: Yes, we know. But, tell me, why are they equal?

LEP Student: It is equal.

Teacher: O.K. They are equal because both number sentences have the same sum. Now, what symbol can we write in the empty square?

Native English-Speaking Student: Equal sign!

Teacher Right! Very good! *(now pointing to an LEP student)* Please write the equal sign inside the square.

LEP Student: *(Obviously not quite sure of what it is she is supposed to do, she goes to the board and writes the answer to each number sentence.)*

Teacher: Good! Tell me what symbol do we write in the *square* to say that this side *(pointing)* is *equal* to this side?

LEP Student: *(Appears embarrassed, lowers her head and does not answer.)*

After class, the teacher wonders how to reach LEP students like the one in this scene. She knows these students are intelligent and eager to learn, but she feels frustrated because she cannot get them to express the mathematical knowledge she thinks they know. Her concern is compounded when she tries to devise ways to teach LEP students whose knowledge of mathematics is also weak.

This is just one illustration of the fact that teaching involves frequent communication between teacher and students. When the dialogue is conducted in a language unfamiliar to the students, difficulties are likely to arise. Morris (1974) describes the nature of the problem:

> The problems of teaching in a second language are accentuated when mathematics is the context of the dialog. This is due essentially to the abstract nature of mathematics and the difficulties which arise in absorbing abstract concepts. Also, the

> language used has to be precise, consis-
> tent, and unambiguous, if mathematical
> ideas are to be explored and described ef-
> fectively. And for dialog to become pos-
> sible, the child must be equipped with a
> basic repertoire of linguistic concepts and
> structures. (p. 52)

Morris' statement underscores the importance of teaching the "special" language skills required for mathematics learning. Mastering "mathematics language" skills is essential for all students, but it is particularly crucial for students learning mathematics in English as a second language (ESL). This chapter discusses the integration of mathematics and language skills in two contexts: (a) incorporating mathematics content into ESL instruction, and (b) incorporating English teaching strategies into mathematics instruction. The following topics will be addressed:

• the nature of the language used in mathematics, including some of the features that may be problematic for LEP students;

• a brief overview of the role language plays in the context of teaching and learning mathematics, with special emphasis on learning mathematics through a second language; and

• suggestions for practical instructional strategies and activities for promoting mathematics and English language skills development with LEP students in both the ESL and the mathematics classroom.

The Language of Mathematics

What is meant by the language of mathematics? How is it different from the language used for everyday communication tasks? The English language represents a universe of language skills, and certain areas of language are used for specific purposes. Natural language, the language used in everyday communication, is one of the components or "subsets" of this universe. The language used to discuss computer technology or that used for scientific topics are two other subsets. Linguistically, these subsets of language are referred to as "registers."

The language register for mathematics is composed of meanings appropriate to the communication of mathematical ideas together with the terms or vocabulary used in expressing these ideas and the structures or sentences in which these terms appear (Halliday, 1975). Like other registers or styles of English, the mathematics register includes unique vocabulary, syntax (sentence structure), semantic properties (truth conditions), and discourse (text) features.

Vocabulary

Mathematics vocabulary includes words that are specific to mathematics, such as *divisor*, *denominator*, *quotient*, and *coefficient*. These words are new to most students. However, the mathematics register also includes natural language, everyday vocabulary that takes on a different meaning in mathematics. These words, such as *equal*, *rational*, *irrational*, *column*, and *table*, must be relearned, this time in a mathematics context, since they have a different meaning in mathematics.

In addition to isolated vocabulary items, the mathematics register uses its special vocabulary to create complex strings of words or phrases. In these phrases, often two or more mathematical concepts combine to form a new concept, compounding the task of comprehending the words. The phrases, *least common multiple*, *negative exponent*, and even an apparently simple phrase such as *a quarter of the apples*, are good examples showing the complexity of mathematical terms.

A subtler and much more difficult aspect of mathematics vocabulary involves the many ways in which the same mathematics operation can be signaled. As students progress through the hierarchy of mathematics skills, manipulation of this vocabulary becomes crucial for understanding the teacher's explanations in class and for solving word problems. Crandall, Dale, Rhodes, and Spanos (1985) have identified groups of lexical items in beginning algebra that indicate certain operations. For example, students must know that addition can be signaled by any of these words:

add	and
plus	sum
combine	increased by

Similarly, subtraction can be signaled by these words:

subtract from	minus
decreased by	differ
less	less than
take away *(a less "sophisticated" term commonly used by children)*	

It is important to remember that when talking about the vocabulary of the mathematics language register (or any register), the meanings of the terms are related to the context in which they are used. Hence it is not enough for students to learn lists of words. They must learn what they mean in a particular mathematical expression. For example, students are taught early in their mathematics education that the word *by* signals multiplication as in the expression *3 multiplied by 10*. However, they later encounter algebraic expressions such as *a number increased by 10* and discover (sometimes the hard way!) that *by* in this case is part of an expression that signals addition. In fact, prepositions in general and the relationships they indicate are critical lexical items in the mathematics register that can cause a great deal of confusion. Another example is *divided by* as opposed to *divided into* (Crandall, Dale, Rhodes, & Spanos, 1985, p. 11).

In addition to words and phrases particular to the mathematics register, some examples of which have been given, there is also the set of mathematical symbols used in expressing mathematical concepts and processes. These items are automatically associated with the symbolic language of mathematics. As symbols that stand for a particular meaning in mathematics, they can be thought of as mathematics vocabulary. The symbols used for operations (adding, dividing, etc.) are the most commonly known. As students move through the mathematics curriculum, the number of symbols used increases, and their meanings become more conceptually dense. Students must learn to relate symbols such as $\geq$, $\leq$, and parentheses and brackets to mathematics concepts or processes (usually themselves couched in mathematics language) and then translate these into everyday language in order to express the mathematical ideas embedded in the symbols.

It is important to remember when discussing mathematical symbols that some symbols play different roles in different countries. In a number of countries, for example, a comma is used to separate whole numbers from decimal parts—the function of the decimal point in the United States, while the decimal point is used as the comma is in the United States, to separate hundreds from thousands, hundred thousands from millions, and so on.

Syntax

The mathematics language register includes, as all registers do, special syntactic structures and special styles of presentation. Knight and Hargis (1977) point out that since mathematics is a study of relationships, comparative structures are an essential and recurring part of "mathematics language." They are difficult structures for many students to master. The following are some examples:

greater than/ less than	as in	all numbers greater than 4
n times as much	as in	Hilda earns six times as much as I do. Hilda earns $40,000. How much do I earn?
as ... as	as in	Wendy is as old as Miguel.

-er than	as in	Miguel is three years older than Frank. Frank is 25. How old is Wendy?

Munro (1979) cites a number of other frequently used structures in mathematics that are also potentially confusing. They include the following structures with examples taken from Crandall, Dale, Rhodes, and Spanos (1985):

numbers used as nouns (rather than adjectives)	as in	Twenty is five times a certain number. What is the number?
prepositions	as in	eight divided *by* four and eight *into* four
	as in	two multiplied *by* itself two times (multiplication) and x exceeds two *by* seven
passive voice	as in	ten *(is) divided by* two.
or,	as in	x *is defined* to be equal to zero.
or,	as in	When 15 *is added* to a number, the result is 21. Find the number.

One of the principal characteristics of the syntax used in a mathematical expression is the lack of one-to-one correspondence between mathematical symbols and the words they represent. For example, if the expression *eight divided by 2* is translated word-for-word in the order in which it is written, the resulting mathematical expression $8\sqrt{2}$ would be incorrect. The correct expression is $2\sqrt{8}$. Similarly, to correctly translate the expression, *the square of the quotient of a and b,* students must know that the first part of the expression, *the square of,* is translated last and that the phrase starting with *quotient* requires the use of parentheses to signal the squaring of the entire quotient. The correct mathematical expression in this case is $(a/b)^2$.

This lack of one-to-one correspondence poses considerable difficulty for students, particularly LEP students, who tend to read and write mathematical sentences (presented either in symbols or in words or both) in the same manner in which they read and write standard orthography (Kessler, Quinn, & Hayes, 1985). Understanding that there is no one-to-one correspondence between mathematics symbols and their English translations becomes crucial for students who are attempting to make progress through the hierarchy of mathematical concepts. In their work with LEP high school and college students in basic algebra classes, Crandall, Dale, Rhodes, and Spanos (1985) have documented recurring errors in translations of the language of word problems into solution equations. They found that students tend to duplicate the surface syntax of the problem statements in their algebraic restatements. For example, students often incorrectly translated the sentence, *The number* a *is five less than the number* b as $a = 5 - b$, when the correct translation should be: $a = b - 5$.

Another major characteristic of the syntax of the language of mathematics is its frequent use of logical connectors. Dawe's (1983) study of LEP students showed that the correct use of logical connectors was the one factor that differentiated those students who could reason mathematically in English from those who could not. The results were consistent for both LEP and native English speakers.

Logical connectors are one linguistic device mathematics texts use to develop and link abstract ideas and concepts. Some of these connectors include *if ... then*, *if and only if*, *because*, *that is*, *for example*, *such that*, *but*, *consequently*, and *either ... or*. As Kessler, Quinn, and Hayes (1985) point out:

> Logical connectors are words or phrases
> which carry out the function of marking a
> logical relationship between two or more
> basic linguistic structures. Primarily,
> logical connectors serve a semantic, co-
> hesive function indicating the nature of
> the relationship between parts of a text.
>
> (p. 14)

When students read mathematics texts, they must

be able to recognize logical connectors and the situations in which they appear. They must know which situation is signaled—similarity, contradiction, cause and effect or reason and result, chronological or logical sequence (Celce-Murcia & Larsen-Freeman, 1983). On the level of syntax, they have to know where logical connectors appear in a sentence (at the beginning, middle, or end of a clause), and they must be aware that some connectors can appear in only one position, while others can appear in two or all three positions, and that change in position can signal a change in meaning.

Examples abound in algebra texts of logical connectors used in definitions and to characterize properties—concepts that students must understand and apply in order to solve algebraic problems. These connectors most often appear in complex statements using both words and symbols, as in the following examples:

> In a beginning algebra text, the *Axiom of Opposites* is stated as:
>
> For every real number a there is a unique real number $-a$, such that
>
> $a + (-a) = 0$ and $(-a) + a = 0$.
>
> The text then offers the following elaboration of the axiom:
>
> 1. If a is a positive number, then $-a$ is a negative number; if a is a negative number, then $-a$ is a positive number; if a is 0, then $-a$ is 0.
>
> 2. The opposite of $-a$ is a; that is, $-(-a) = a$.
>> (Dolciani & Wooton, 1970, p. 77)

It is not hard to imagine native-English-speaking students having difficulty piecing together the logical statements in this section of text. Clearly, LEP students might have even more difficulty with it.

This complex example is taken from a level of

This complex example is taken from a level of mathematics that most students generally do not face until they are at least in junior high school. It is important to note that LEP students' ability to manipulate logical connectors appears to be tied into a developmental sequence. It is very possible that younger LEP students categorically have more problems with logical connectors than older students (Piaget, 1926; Tritch, 1984, as quoted in Kessler, Quinn, & Hayes, 1985). Younger students often seem mystified by the use of logical connectors such as *if* in relatively simple word problems. Some students may, for example, have considerable difficulty solving the following problem stated using a hypothetical situation signaled by *if*:

If Frank can type one page in 20 minutes, how much time will it take him to type two pages?

However, the same students may be able to solve the problem when it is stated using a declarative sentence, as in:

Frank types one page in 20 minutes. How much time does it take him to type two pages?

Semantics

The preceding discusssion shows that correctly manipulating the special vocabulary and phrases and the word order found in "mathematics language" is intricately tied to students' ability to infer the correct mathematical meaning from the language. Making inferences in "mathematics language" often depends on the language user's knowledge of how reference is indicated. In algebra, for example, the correct solution of a word problem often hinges on the ability to identify key words and to determine the other words in the problem to which the key words are linked (i.e., knowing how to determine the referents of key words). Problems involving *the number*, *a number*, and the like require such inferencing. For example:

Five times a number is two more than ten times

To solve this problem, students must realize that *a number* and *the number* refer to the same quantity.

The sum of two numbers is 77. If the first number is 10 times the other, find the number.

In this problem, students must know that they are dealing with two numbers. Further, they must know that the way reference is used in the problem links each number with information about it, so that *the first number* and the information given about it refers to one of those numbers; and *the other* refers to the second of the two numbers, *the number* whose value the problem asks the student to find. Finally, students must know that the translation from the words of the problem into the symbolic representation of the solution equation will be based on only one variable and that each of the two numbers will be expressed in terms of that one variable. Given all this, the correct translation and solution of this problem would be:

Phrase	Symbolic Translation
first number	$10x$
second number	x
sum	77

Therefore, on the basis of information from the problem:

$$11x = 77 \quad \text{and}$$
$$x = 7$$

A common mistake is for students to write solution equations with two *different* variables. Not surprisingly, because they see no relationship between the two equations, they cannot solve the problem.

These examples point out another reference feature of the language of mathematics, specifically to the language of algebra: the referents of variables. Identifying variables' referents is essential to correctly translating the words of a problem into the symbols of its solution equation and vice versa. Variables stand for the *number* of persons or things, *not* the persons or things themselves. The following classic word problem illustrates this point:

> There are five times as many students as professors in the mathematics depart-ment. Write an equation that represents this statement.

Many students typically write the incorrect equation $5s = p,$ which follows the literal word order of the natural language sentence and uses s to represent "students" and p to represent "professors." The correct equation is $5p = s,$ which can be determined only if students know that the variable s (or any other variable they choose to use) must represent the *number* of students and that the variable p must represent the *number* of professors. This kind of "reversal error" has been the subject of investigation by a number of researchers interested in the language of mathematics, including Clement (1981) and Mestre, Gerace, & Lockhead (1982). Firsching (1982) points out that recurring reversal errors could result from students' previous repeated exposure in "beginning"-level mathematics to word problems that feature a one-to-one correspondence between words and symbol. Experienced with such word problems, they incorrectly expect that all problems can be solved in the same manner.

Discourse Features

On a level above vocabulary and syntax, known in linguistics as the *discourse* level, mathematics language also has distinctive characteristics. Loosely defined, mathematics discourse refers to the "chunks" of language—sentences or groups of sentences or paragraphs—that function together as *textual units, each* with a specific meaning and purpose in mathematics. The definition of the communicative property of addition or the explanation of this property in a mathematics textbook are examples of mathematics discourse or "texts." Any word problem is an example of a specialized type of mathematics discourse or text.

All of the lexical, syntactic, and semantic features of "mathematics language" discussed earlier can be considered discourse features of a mathematics text. But instead of looking at isolated features from the "bottom up," discourse views how all the distinctive features of a mathematics text work from the "top down" to form a cohesive, coherent unit that communicates a particular mathematics meaning. This meaning is expressed not as a result of the simple sum of all of its lexical, syntactic, and semantic features but rather as something above and beyond these features. To understand a unit of mathematical discourse, students must not only be proficient in "mathematics language," but they must also have a background in mathematics in order to construct the context needed to process cognitively complex information. At the discourse level, the integration of language and mathematics skills is essential for total comprehension.

Mathematics discourse, especially written discourse, presents considerable difficulties for many students, native English speakers as well as LEP students. Unlike natural language, mathematics texts lack redundancy or paraphrase. Bye (1975) has enumerated a number of additional characteristics of mathematical discourse found in the language of mathematics textbooks. According to his analysis, written mathematics texts:

- are conceptually packed;
- have high density;
- require up-and-down as well as left-to-right eye movements;
- require a reading rate adjustment because they must be read more slowly than natural language texts;
- require multiple readings;
- use numerous symbolic devices such as charts and graphs; and

- contain a great deal of technical language with

- contain a great deal of technical language with precise meaning.

These language features, when combined with the mathematics content of the written text, require the student to apply mathematics concepts, procedures, and applications they have already learned. (Students with a weak mathematics background as well as poor language skills are doubly handicapped here.) The student must also recognize *which* previously learned mathematics concepts, procedures, or applications must be applied to the text at hand. In addition, the student must have had enough experience with mathematics texts to know when everyday background knowledge should be applied to the reading comprehension process and when it must be suspended. Finally, the student must be familar with (have had experience with) the processes involved in mathematical thinking.

Mathematical word problems provide some of the more cogent examples of mathematics discourse features at work, along with illustrations of the difficulties these features present to LEP students, who are for the most part unfamiliar with mathematics discourse in English (and sometimes in any language).

Kessler, Quinn, and Hayes (1985) offer the example of the following word problem, which many of their second-grade LEP students could not solve correctly:

> Sue has 32 cards. She gave Jim 15 cards. How many cards does Sue have?

The authors report that many students responded with 15 rather than 17. They theorize that these students may not have been familiar with the representative function of word problems, by which they would have perceived that having 32 cards and giving 15 of them away represents or sets up a mathematics situation, not the beginning of a narrative or story.

It could be argued that the language of this problem is unclear and ambiguous. Sophisticated problem-solvers have learned how to deal with such ambiguity because they know that the function of the language of word problems is to direct them toward a mathematical solution. They suspend the natural tendency to demand details that they might normally require for reading narrative texts. Consider the following problem, for example:

> Food expenses take 26% of the average family's income. A family makes $700 a month. How much is spent on food?

Students who can solve this problem generally are not bothered by the fact that the problem does not specify directly the amount that is being asked for, that is, the amount per month? the amount per year? Since one time reference occurs in the problem—*a month*—students who know how word problems work infer that they must find the amount spent per month. Students who are not proficient in the language of word problems probably would demand a paraphrase or repetition of the time reference to clarify the problem question. It is clear that LEP students, often literal readers at the early stages of their English development, would have grave difficulties with word problem texts such as this one.

It appears that good problem-solvers are the students who can discover the discourse properties of word problems that provide them with both a real-world context and a mathematics context in which to approach the problem. Further, Kessler, Quinn, and Hayes (1985) point out that proficient problem-solvers "make use of language for thinking purposes in a real world context" (p. 18). Students need to acquire the skills to integrate complex linguistic and mathematical processes in order to be good problem-solvers.

The Role of Language Learning in Mathematics

The previous section lists, by no means exhaustively, the linguistic items and language skills required for mathematics learning. Identifying the special style or register of mathematics is the first step toward de-

students that integrate language and mathematics. The next step must be to provide a broad framework or a perspective from which to view how language in general and mathematics language in particular relates to mathematics learning.

Language Proficiency and Mathematics Achievement

Results from extensive research with monolingual English speakers point to a close relationship between language proficiency and mathematics achievement. Research reviews by Aiken (1971), Corle (1974), and Suydam (1982) reveal high positive correlations between (English) reading ability and mathematics achievement.

Research with students learning mathematics in ESL is limited. However, the research that is available shows similar positive correlations between language skills and mathematics achievement. Cossio (1978) found a positive correlation between mathematics achievement and second language ability. Duran (1980) also found a strong positive correlation between the reading comprehension scores of Puerto Rican college students and their performance on deductive reasoning problems in English and in Spanish, with a similar pattern aross both languages. Cuevas (1984) has shown that language is a factor both in the learning and the assessment of mathematics.

Although the exact relationship between language and mathematics is not clearly understood, results of available research certainly point toward close interaction. On one level, it could be said that proficiency in the language in which mathematics is taught, particularly reading proficiency, is a prerequisite for mathematics achievement. The reading of mathematics texts and the solving of mathematics word problems obviously depends on a prerequisite language proficiency. The student must be able to read the text in order to understand the mathematics concept or process expressed in it. By the same token, a student must be able to first read a word problem before attempting to solve it. However, being able to read the text or the problem does not guarantee understanding of the concept or process or being able to solve the problem.

Early research by Macnamara (1966) appears to bear this hypothesis out. In his studies of English-Irish bilingual students, Macnamara found that students had greater difficulty solving word problems in Irish, their weaker (second) language, than in English, their stronger (first) language, even when they knew all the words and structures of the problems. Macnamara hypothesized that his subjects lacked what he called a "good grasp" of the weaker language. When closely examined, Macnamara's concept of "grasp" of the language appears to encompass the ability to use language to interpret the problem-solving task.

At this juncture, however, knowledge of and experience with the mathematics concepts and processes become critical. It is very likely that these factors will ultimately *predict* success in mathematics. In particular, the ability to think mathematically appears to be the crucial element in mathematics achievement. It may be at this cognitive and metacognitive level that language and mathematics are most intricately related.

Mathematical Thinking

Kessler, Quinn, and Hayes (1985) present a strong argument that the role of mathematical thinking and metacognition must be considered when discussing the mathematics performance of LEP students. These authors discuss Burton's model (1984) of mathematics learning, which involves not only the cognitive tasks of carrying out particular operations, processes, and dynamics connected with the study of mathematics, but also a special style of thinking that is different from the body of knowledge (content and techniques) traditionally identified as mathematics. This style of thinking involves metacognition, which Garofalo and Lester (1985) define as "choosing and planning what to do and monitoring what is being done" (p. 164). Metacognition, then, as Kessler, Quinn, and Hayes (1985) point out, refers to "both awareness of thinking and regulation of thinking. In mathematics (as in all learning), both of these factors affect the outcome of cognitive activities" (p. 3).

Affective factors are also involved in the process of mathematical thinking. Students' mathematical thinking and metacognition must be driven by a curiosity and a willingness to investigate the unknown. Students must also be patient and persistent. These qualities, together with a knowledge of mathematics concepts, operations, and processes, no doubt all contribute to success in mathematics.

Learning Mathematics Through a Second Language

In school, students must use language, written and spoken, to express their thoughts and to demonstrate their understanding and mastery of academic tasks. Simply put, language is the vehicle of learning and instruction. As Cummins (1981) has theorized, the language used for academic tasks is quite different from the language used for basic communication. Cummins' "basic interpersonal communication skills" (BICS) refer to a proficiency in the context-embedded language found in face-to-face conversation, where speakers rely strongly on extralinguistic and situational cues for meaning.

Cognitive academic language proficiency (CALP), on the other hand, refers to a proficiency in the context-reduced language related to cognitive tasks. With CALP, meaning is inferred essentially from the linguistic or literacy-related features of the spoken or written text. The meaning is more or less complex depending on the level of cognitive demand presented by the academic task being expressed through the language.

Cummins argues that CALP is cross-lingual, that is, students can acquire CALP, part of what he calls "a common underlying proficiency," via any language as long as they have reached a certain level or "threshold" of proficiency in the language. Once acquired, CALP can be accessed and used via any language, again once the threshold level of proficiency in the language has been reached.

The concept of threshold in Cummins' model may have important implications for LEP students faced with the task of learning mathematics and other academic subjects. If LEP students already possess a threshold proficiency in CALP (in mathematics, for example, learned through their first language), they have a basis on which to develop CALP for mathematics through their second language. Hence their chances to succeed in academic tasks, in this case mathematics tasks, are enhanced, given enough time and motivation to learn their second language.

However, it may be the case that LEP students who have little or no CALP in their first language will have considerable difficulty developing CALP through their second language. Although it is not explicitly stated by Cummins, their difficulties may have to do not only with learning second language skills but also with learning the cognitive, academic content expressed through the second language. Thus the threshold that LEP students must reach is both a certain minimal level of language skills and a certain minimal knowledge of the academic area.

Dawe's work (1983, 1984) with bilingual students in mathematical reasoning appears to agree with research conducted by Mestre, Gerace, and Lockhead (1982) with Hispanic engineering students in college algebra courses. These researchers report that Hispanic students were much more likely than nonminority students to misinterpret word problems in English and that slower reading speed and comprehension contributed significantly to a greater number of problems not being completed (and consequently "missed") in the word problem tests they administered. Mestre (1984) recommends that problem-solving instruction for Hispanics (and other LEP students) should therefore include extensive practice emphasizing speed and accuracy in translating the language of word problems into mathematical notation. He argues that LEP students who are given a chance to grapple with problems that demand considerable linguistic processing would learn how to get information from a problem and set it up correctly.

In summary, the role of language in learning is not

yet clear, although it is likely that its role is crucial in the following ways.

1. There appears to be a high correlation between reading skills and mathematics achievement, particularly when the tasks involve reading texts or solving word problems. Preliminary research evidence appears to indicate that this correlation may be even stronger for LEP students performing tasks in ESL.

2. On a "deeper" level, language works as a mediator for mathematical thinking and metacognition. Whether the thinking defines the language or the language defines the thinking remains to be answered. Probably both occur. The important point is that mathematical thinking, mediated by linguistic processes, is a prerequisite for mathematics achievement.

3. LEP students who must learn mathematics through their second language must reach a minimal level (Cummins' threshold) of proficiency in the cognitive, academic skills required of mathematics and in the language skills used to express the mathematical skills.

4. The language used in mathematics is intricately connected to the mathematical concepts, processes, and applications it expresses. Therefore, mathematics instruction, particularly for LEP students learning in their second language, should integrate mathematics and language skills.

Learning a Second Language Through Mathematics

Another aspect of the relationship between language and mathematics is critical for LEP students. Mathematics instruction for LEP students can be a source of opportunities to acquire and learn English, their second language. In other words, mathematics can be a language-learning experience in both the mathematics and the ESL class.

Recent research and practical experience appear to suggest that the forms, functions, and uses of language can be best acquired and learned in context. Second language acquisition theory, notably that of Krashen (1982), points to the importance of context to provide language experiences, or "input," that students can comprehend. It seems obvious that the language input students need most in school must come from experiences from their academic subject courses.

Traditionally, mathematics has not been one of the subject areas educators use to provide second language experiences and practice for LEP students. It is possible that the myth that mathematics requires minimal language proficiency may have kept mathematics from being a logical choice as the academic content base of second language activities. Perhaps the fact that many language teachers feel unprepared and reluctant to get involved with any topic related to mathematics has also affected the "popularity" of choosing mathematics content.

It is essential, however, that the classroom environment in which ESL is taught through mathematics content be carefully structured so that second language acquisition can occur. For both the ESL and the mathematics classroom, this means that instructional activities should promote second language development through a natural, subconscious process in which the focus is not on language per se but on *communicating* the concepts, processes, and applications of mathematics.

Mohan (1986) points out that an instructional environment that promotes second (and first) language development must be carefully structured to provide students with a range of opportunities to communicate subject matter. His general framework for teaching language and content suggests that ESL activities based on mathematics content make use of graphics, manipulatives, and other hands-on concrete experiences that clarify and reinforce meanings in mathematics communicated through language.

It is not enough, however, to include instructional activities that provide linguistic and nonlinguistic enforcement for communicating mathematical ideas. As with any instruction, teachers must constantly monitor their students for comprehension, which may require special attention in mathematics given the cognitive complexity of many mathematics tasks and the tendency for mathematics to be a silent, individual activity (Cazden, 1979). Teachers therefore need to provide both quality input tailored to the language and mathematics levels of their students *and* ample opportunity for students to respond (i.e., *talk*), again commensurate with their level of language and mathematics proficiency. Given the cognitive demands of mathematics tasks, teachers must also provide students with extensive and varied experiences in which to apply the mathematical thinking techniques and the metacognitive behaviors (i.e., the self-monitoring of mathematical processes) they will need to develop to be mathematics achievers.

Whenever possible, instructional activities, in both the ESL and the mathematics classroom, should be built on students' real-life experiences and prior knowledge of mathematics, and offer situations in which students can interact with the teacher and fellow students (both LEP and English-speaking). Such activities stimulate both second language acquisition and learning. Wilson, De Avila, and Intili (1982) and De Avila and Duncan (1984) have shown that when LEP students are provided with a classroom environment organized around interactive activities, they can acquire both mathematics and English simultaneously. De Avila's program provides hands-on experiments that foster critical thinking skills for mathematics and science. Because the activities naturally emphasize process, they lend themselves well to promoting verbal interaction. Similar evidence for the simultaneous development of language and mathematics and science can be found in studies by Kessler and Quinn (1980, 1984), Quinn and Kessler (1984), and Rodriguez and Bethel (1983).

Affective factors also play a crucial role in the language acquisition process described here. Many students, not just LEP students, decide for one reason or another that they "are not good in mathematics." For many LEP students faced with the formidable task of learning mathematics through a second language, mathematics instruction can be doubly traumatic. Mathematics teachers can do much to reduce the trauma by giving LEP students opportunities to experience success in mathematics through activities they can understand. Positive experiences in mathematics build on themselves and can consequently lower what Krashen (1982) calls "the affective filter" in language learning. The result is that LEP students find themselves learning mathematics, while at the same time they are acquiring language skills used both in everyday communication and in the academic setting of mathematics.

Results from the work of Hayes and Bahruth (1985) and Hayes, Bahruth, and Kessler (1985) bear this observation out. These researchers report extraordinary progress in fifth-grade LEP students' English reading skills as a result of extensive experience in reading and writing their own mathematics word problems. Both studies emphasize that students' success was due not only to exposure to great quantities of interesting and relevant language input, but also to the students' changes in attitudes toward school and learning.

It should be emphasized that ESL teachers can design mathematics activities as simple as learning to read and write the names of numbers in English to more complex work such as talking about how to solve word problems. If such activities are tailored to the language and mathematics proficiencies of the students, they will have numerous oportunities to experience success in completing both language and mathematics tasks, and they will be able to do so in a less threatening atmosphere than the mathematics classroom, where they are often at a disadvantage both in language and in mathematics. It is not unrealistic to think that positive experiences (not to mention the mathematics and language skills learned) in mathematics/language activities in an ESL setting can be carried over to the regular mathematics classroom.

Instructional Strategies

The background that teachers need in order to develop strategies and activities that integrate language and mathematics skills for LEP students has been presented in the previous sections. In this section, suggestions are given for the development of instructional activities. Two instructional settings will be addressed: (a) the mathematics classroom, and (b) the ESL classroom.

Language-Based Strategies for the Mathematics Classroom

The mathematics curriculum at any grade level is generally composed of four basic areas: concepts, computation, applications, and problem-solving. For the purpose of illustrating the differences in language requirements that exist in these four basic mathematics areas, following are two short "lessons."

Lesson 1: Statistics—The Concept of Mean

Teacher: We have on the board two lists of numbers; let's say the numbers represent scores on tests. Add the scores in the first list or distribution; after you have obtained a sum, divide the total by the number of scores in the list. Let's see, first what is the total?

Student 1: *(Gives the correct total.)*

Teacher: Now, what is the result of the division?

Student 2: *(Gives the correct quotient.)*

Teacher: Repeat the same operation with the second list or distribution. *(Answers are checked before proceeding.)* Please tell me where in each distribution the final quotient is located. *(Students locate the quotient or "average" on the board.)*

Teacher: Give me a word or expression that tells where this number is in the distribution of scores.

Student 3: Middle.

Student 4: Center.

Student 5: The other scores are around this answer.

Teacher: I see we pretty much agree that this result or quotient is somewhere in the "center" of each distribution. We call this number a "measure of central tendency." We know that the calculations we did had to do with the average of each of the distributions. Can someone give me a definition of "average"? *(The students give a number of plausible definitions.)* In statistics, this average has a special name. It is called the "mean."

Lesson 2: Statistics—The Computation of Standard Deviation

Teacher: *(The students have previously been presented with the concept of standard deviation.)* Now we are ready to learn the sets involved in the computation of the standard deviation of the distribution.

First, subtract the mean of the distribution from each of the scores in the distribution.

Second, square each of these differences.

Third, add these squares.

Fourth, divide the sum of the squares by the number of scores in the distribution.

Fifth, take the square root of this quotient.

(The students have followed each of the steps and have responded with answers to each as the teacher developed the algorithm.)

In analyzing these two sample lessons, mathematics teachers can readily distiguish the mathematics content: Lesson 1 deals with the development of a concept, in this case, the idea of arithmetic mean; Lesson 2 covers the presentation of the algorithm to compute the standard deviation. As for the language demands of the two lessons, teachers can observe a fairly clear difference in the "scripts" for each lesson. Generally, Lesson 1 contains a larger percentage of natural language, while Lesson 2 emphasizes the technical vocabulary and structures of the mathematics register. The nature of the mathematics content in each lesson defines the kind of language used to teach it. The introduction of a concept requires the teacher to communicate ideas in language familar to the students (i.e., through natural language) to facilitate comprehension. In the development of algorithmic procedures, the instructor assumes understanding of the concept and uses very "technical language" from the mathematics register to present the steps involved in the computation of the standard deviation.

Second Language Approach to Mathematics Skills (SLAMS)

Mathematics teachers can start with general observations on the language content of mathematics tasks (such as the ones just given) and from them develop an expanded mathematics/language approach for LEP students that includes a language component. Cuevas (1981, 1984) has developed such an approach called Second Language Approach to Mathematics Skills (SLAMS), which incorporates language development activities into the "regular" mathematics lessons planned by teachers. This approach was initially developed for grade K through 12, but can be applied to any level of mathematics instruction. It is based on the assumption that in order for a student to master the mathematics concepts presented in class, the language of the concepts must be addressed and mastered. It is also assumed that by teaching the language together with the content, understanding of the material will be facilitated (Cuevas, Mann, & McClung, 1985).

The approach is composed of two strands, one focusing on mathematics content and the other emphasizing related language skills. The activities developed for each strand are based on identified instructional objectives from the mathematics curriculum.

The Content Strand

The content strand encompasses strategies for analysis and diagnosis of mathematics skills, followed by preventive or prescriptive activities. Since this approach follows a "standard" diagnostic-prescriptive model for teaching, its components are described only briefly here.

1. *Analysis of Concept/Skills:* This component deals with what needs to be taught, i.e., the basic mathematics concepts and skills determined by the instructional objectives. At this point, the teacher may also wish to analyze prerequisite skills necessary for mastery of the objectives.

2. *Diagnosis*: This process encompasses assessment (formal and informal) of the level of skills mastery and/or the extent and nature of mathematical errors. Diagnosis must involve data-collection activities in which the teacher focuses on patterns of behavior. These patterns are essential for the instructional decisions made in the next components of the diagnostic-prescriptive process. As a result of the analysis of the instructional objective(s), the teacher needs to ask: "Does the student have the prerequisite skills necessary for mastery of the mathematics objective(s)?" For example, before teaching how to apply the basic arithmetic operations to problem situations dealing with money, the teacher needs to know to what degree the students have mastered the operation(s) they are being asked to use.

3. *Preventive Strategies:* This component addresses the activities designed to review or reinforce skills that are prerequisite to the mathematics objective(s) being taught.

4. *Lesson:* Based on the student's strengths and

weaknesses, the teacher develops instructional activities designed to teach selected mathematics concepts or to develop certain skills. In constructing these activities, care should be taken to select from various approaches such as the use of manipulatives, small-group work, individual tasks, and tutorial sessions with other students as tutors.

As is common in a diagnostic-prescriptive approach, an assessment is made of the level of student mastery of the mathematics content presented in class. The cycle is then repeated or other activities are designed if remediation is necessary.

The Language Strand

The language strand of the SLAMS model follows a path parallel to the content strand. The components of the language strand include:

1. *Analysis of the Language Used:* For this component, teachers need to be aware that at least two languages are present in the mathematics curriculum: the "objective language," or mathematics register, and natural language. Vocabulary and other terms the teacher feels are important in the communication of ideas to the student must be identified. For example, in a word problem such as, "If Marta buys 3 pencils at $0.15 each, how much change will she receive from $1.00?" students need to determine which terms and what syntactic and other textual clues will indicate the correct sequence of operations.

2. *Diagnosis of Language Skills:* On the basis of the language skills identified in the first component, the teacher must answer the following questions:

    a. Does the student recognize the symbols/terms that pertain to the skill?

    b. Can the student pronounce them? Write them?

    c. Can the student define the terms used?

    d. Is the student knowledgeable of the structures used so that ideas and relationships are understood?

3. *Preventive Language Strategies:* Many LEP students have received mathematics instruction in their native language and are proficient in the mathematics register of that language. Preventive language activities could focus on:

    a. a review of the mathematics content, presented this time in the students' native language;

    b. structured ESL activities designed to increase the students' level of competence in the English-language skills needed to master the mathematics content in English.

4. *Lesson:* Instructional language activities for mathematics should involve listening comprehension, verbal production, and reading and writing of the language features identified by the teacher. *These activities must be incorporated as an integral part of the mathematics content lesson.*

The mathematics/language approch of SLAMS outlined here is recommended for mathematics teachers in general. The approach provides a framework for adapting activities the teacher needs to develop to focus on the language needs of LEP students. As can be seen in Figure 1.1, mathematics teachers must analyze each mathematical task into mathematics and language skills. Instructional activities that integrate both kinds of skills must then be devised for the prescriptive and evaluation phases of the approach.

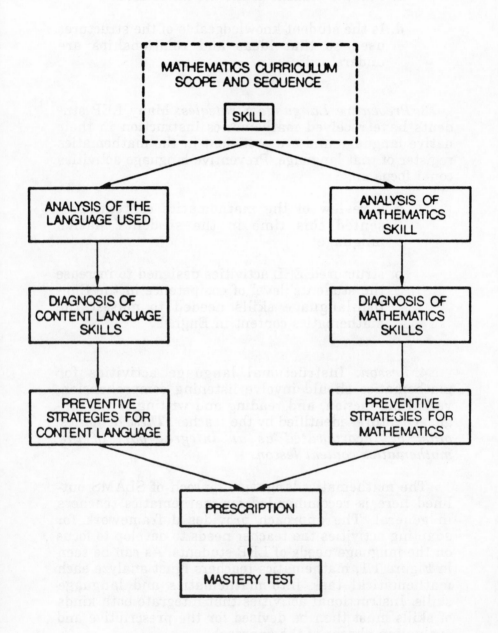

Figure 1.1. *Second Language Approach*
to *Mathematics Skills* (SLAMS) instructional model.

English Language Skills for Basic Algebra

The model suggested by *SLAMS* provides a general approach for integrating mathematics and language skills in the mathematics classsroom. Using this approach, teachers can develop a sequence of language-based mathematics activities for LEP students. (These are the materials suggested for the prescriptive step of the *SLAMS* model.) One such set of materials (Crandall, forthcoming) was developed to assist LEP college students in basic algebra. The mathematics content and the language-based activities stem from extensive research at a number of postsecondary institutions in the United States in which the authors observed basic algebra classes, interviewed LEP students and mathematics faculty and reviewed mathematics textbooks and curricula. The resulting materials are the collaborative effort of language and mathematics specialists. The five units of activities include four units addressing the following topics from beginning algebra: (a) numerical and algebraic expressions, (b) equations and inequalities, (c) word problems, and (d) definitions and theorems. The fifth unit is a glossary of basic algebraic terms. Examples appear as Figures 1.2 through 1.5.

TUTOR PAGE	STUDENT PAGE
TUTOR: Read each algebraic expression to your partner. Your partner will repeat. Listen to see that he or she repeats correctly.	STUDENT: Look at the algebraic expressions below. Listen as your tutor reads the expression. Repeat after your tutor or the tape.
Example:	Example:
Student sees: $x + 2$ You say: "x plus two" Student repeats: "x plus two"	You see: $x + 2$ You hear: "x plus two" You repeat: "x plus two"

Figure 1.2. Working with numerical and algebraic expressions.

The first four units are organized to supplement and reinforce traditional activities conducted in beginning algebra courses. They are designed to be used by students in pairs, in a peer-tutoring approach that enables students to take on the roles of tutor and tutee. In this way, students can work one-on-one in tutoring sessions in the mathematics classroom or in tutorial centers. Since the materials follow a progression from easy to difficult for both mathematics and language proficiency, they provide students working in pairs of small groups with numerous opportunities for the debate and discussion that are crucial for the development of mathematical thinking. The instructional environment thus created can offer students extensive "comprehensible mathematics/language input." Algebra teachers have also used the units with entire classes to introduce or reinforce topics.

TUTOR PAGE

TUTOR: Look at the equations below. Certain steps are left out and explanations are given for the missing steps. Listen as your partner fills in the missing steps in the equations by reading the explanations. Check his or her answers with the underlined answers below.

STUDENT PAGE

STUDENT: In the equations that follow, certain steps are left out, and explanations are given for the missing steps. Fill in the missing steps in the equations by reading the corresponding explanations. Then read your answer out loud to your tutor. Observe how the equation is solved in the example.

Example: Solve $7a - 2 = 3a + 9$

Steps

$7a - 2 = 3a + 9$

$7a - 2 + (-3a) = 3a + 9 + (-3a)$

Explanation for Steps

The given problem.

Add $-3a$ to both sides to isolate the variable on one side.

. . .

Figure 1.3. Working with equations and inequalities

Although peer tutoring is the ideal framework for these materials, they can also be used by students individually, with the "tutor" sections serving as answer sheets and a check on students' progress. The materials have been used in this manner as homework supplements and as materials for individual practice in tutorial centers.

TUTOR PAGE

TUTOR: Listen to your partner read and answer the following paraphrase and inference questions. He or she should circle the letter of the correct answer. When he or she is finished, check the answers and give explanations for those that are incorrect.

1. Which of the following is closest in meaning to the subtraction equation?

A) No. Check the definition again.

B) YES

STUDENT PAGE

STUDENT: Read the following paraphrase and inference questions out loud. Circle the letter of the correct answer. Refer to the definition above.

1. Which of the following is closest in meaning to the subtraction equation?

A) a over b, less c over b, is the difference between a-c into b.

B) a over b, less c over b, is equal to the difference between a and c over b.

Figure 1.4. Understanding definitions and theorems

The glossary offers students a reference tool for basic algebra that provides definitions of algebra vocabulary; a list of symbols along with their names, functions, and the vocabulary and phrases that express them; definitions and examples of the types of numbers; and finally, a list of words and phrases commonly used in typical algebra word problems. The glossary's entries were carefully constructed to provide both the technical language that students would find in their mathematics texts and definitions and explanations written in natural language. In this way students can understand the meanings of terms, symbols, and expressions as they are exposed to the technical language they ultimately need to learn to function in algebra class.

TERM	EXAMPLE	MEANING
Commutative property of multiplication	4 x 8 = 8 x 4	If a and b are integers, then $ab = ba$. Hint: The word <u>commute</u> means to exchange, so the integers <u>exchange</u> positions in this property.
complex number	-3 + 4i	Complex numbers have the form $a + bi$, where a and b are real numbers. The a is called the real part and the bi is called the imaginary part.
composite number	4, 6, 8, 9 ...	A counting number that is <u>not</u> prime.
counting number	1, 2, 3, 4 ...	the numbers we use to count with. They are also called natural numbers.

. . .

ADDITION

Sym-bol	Related Words	Examples	Explanation
+	add addition	3 + 4	"3 + 4" means add 3 and 4; do the operation of addition.
	plus, increased by	"3 + 4" may be read "3 plus 4" or "3 increased by 4"	The symbol for addition is the plus sign: +
	sum	"Find the sum of 3 plus 4"	The answer to an addition problem is called the *sum* of the two numbers. CAUTION: Do not confuse the word <u>sum</u> (requiring addition) with the word <u>product</u> (requiring multi-plication).

. . .

Figure 1.5. A glossary for basic algebra.

Finally, it is important to note that language-based mathematics materials such as these can be used by all students, not just LEP students. Since acquiring the mathematics register appears to be difficult for most students, the algebra activities designed to teach the meanings and functions of mathematics language are probably beneficial for any student.

Mathematics-Based Strategies for the ESL Classroom

Many of the mathematics/language activities suggested for the mathematics classroom can be adapted for the ESL classroom. However, the ultimate goal of these activities is different. In the mathematics class, the goal is to learn mathematics, but in the ESL classroom, the goal of every activity is to foster language acquisition and learning. As discussed earlier in the chapter and elsewhere in this volume, the introduction of content-based ESL activities serves to shift the conscious focus of ESL students from the mechanics of language learning to the function of language, that is, the communication of meaning. In academic settings, then, one of the contexts ESL instructors can use to teach students how language communicates academic meaning (i.e., to teach functional English) is that of mathematics.

To develop mathematics-content language activities for the ESL classroom, ESL teachers must ascertain the mathematics objectives and skills of the mathematics courses their LEP students are (or will be) required to complete along with some idea of the mathematics their students already know. Unless the ESL or bilingual teacher is also the students' mathematics teacher, this task requires the advice and assistance of mathematics instructors, particularly those who teach the same LEP students who are in ESL classes.

Together, mathematics and ESL teachers must assess LEP students' mathematics needs and skills. This diagnosis is then incorporated into an assessment of students' language proficiency. The resulting profile provides ESL teachers with an overall picture of the two sets of skills (mathematics and language) on which they can develop mathematics-based language activities.

At this point, it is probably obvious that ESL teachers who want to incorporate mathematics content into ESL learning are faced with the sizable task of compiling a mathematics-based section for their ESL curriculum, a curriculum that is already packed full with language (listening, speaking, reading, and writing) objectives and activities. The key to making this task manageable must be in selecting which mathematics content to include. Depending on the goals of the ESL program, on the basis of student needs, ESL teachers can select mathematics content according to two broadly defined approaches. The objective of the first approach is to present a complete sequence of mathematics tasks. The result of this approach is a mathematics component of an ESL curriculum that concentrates on teaching academic English. The objective of the second approach is to include a few mathematics-based activities among other more traditional second language learning activities. The approach results in an ESL curriculum that introduces but does not necessarily concentrate on the academic language used for mathematics tasks.

A discussion of each of these mathematics-based approaches for ESL follows. It should be noted that these two approaches are two extremes of a continuum. ESL teachers can develop many variations of the approaches that fall somewhere in the middle, according to the needs of their students and the time and resources available.

Developing a Sequenced Component of Math-Based Language Activities for ESL

If ESL teachers find, after consultation with mathematics instructors and the students themselves, that their LEP students are having serious difficulties with particular parts of the mathematics curriculum, the ESL teacher may choose to include mathematics-based language activities sequenced to the mathematics curriculum as a regular part of ESL instruction. The following suggestions are offered.

• ESL teachers, again with the help of mathematics instructors, need to analyze the objectives and activities of the mathematics curriculum identified as difficult to determine the language features that contribute to students' problems. These features and the mathematics content from which they originate will form the basis for mathematics-content language activities.

• ESL teachers again must narrow down the mathematics content to a component that can be realistically

TUTOR PAGE	STUDENT PAGE
TUTOR: Listen to the sentence your partner reads. Be sure he or she reads <u>the number</u> correctly. The sentences are below. The numbers are underlined.	STUDENT: Read the following sentences out loud. Be sure to say the numbers correctly.
Example: There were <u>five hundred</u> people at the meeting.	Example: You read: There were 500 people at the meeting.
1. His father is <u>six</u> feet tall.	1. His father is 6 feet tall.
2. The electric bill was <u>three hundred (and) thirteen dollars!</u>	2. The electric bill was $313!
3. My car holds <u>twelve point five</u> (twelve and five tenths) gallons of gas.	3. My car holds 12.5 gallons of gas.
4. There are <u>five thousand two hundred (and) eighty</u> feet in a mile.	4. There are 5,280 feet in a mile.
. . .	
7. My phone number is <u>two-three-two-four-five-one-six</u>.	7. My phone number is 232-4516.
8. Over <u>one million</u> people live in New York.	8. Over 1,000,000 people live in New York.

Figure 1.6. Math-based ESL lesson: Using numbers in everyday contexts.

incorporated into the daily schedule. Ideally, mathematics and ESL teachers should work together to prioritize all the mathematics areas identified and to ensure that the mathematics material students need most will be covered.

• To date, few materials specifically offer a component of mathematics-based ESL activities. In the absence of sets of ESL materials dedicated to mathematics, ESL teachers must adapt and compile (perhaps with the help of interested mathematics specialists) sequences of activities for the particular areas of mathematics (general mathematics, algebra, geometry, etc.) their LEP students are studying.

Figure 1.6 (p. 45) shows how mathematics/language materials originally written for mathematics classrooms can be adapted for ESL instruction for high school or college students. The example is based on activities from the series of materials described earlier, which were primarily written for use in algebra classes. The mathematics content comes from the first unit, which treats numerical and algebraic expressions.

The example in Figure 1.6 illustrates how parts of mathematics-based language activities can be incorporated into the regular daily or weekly schedule of ESL instruction—with efforts made to parallel the objectives being addressed in the mathematics classroom. It is also possible to build an entire sequence of mathematics-based language activities as a type of English for special purposes (ESP) section of an ESL course.

Developing Problem-Solving Activities That Promote Second Language Acquisition

In many cases, ESL programs cannot devote an entire component of the ESL curriculum to mathematics content. The brief outline given earlier shows that such a process requires extended time and effort on the part of ESL and mathematics instructors, especially since materials are needed. In addition, many ESL programs may find that their LEP students may not need intensive instruction in mathematics-based language learning either because they already have a sound base in mathematics in their native language or they have strong support from their regular mathematics teachers, who pay special attention to the language needs of students in their classes.

Even if students are doing relatively well in regular mathematics classes, ESL teachers may still want to include some kind of stimulating, thought-provoking mathematics-based language instruction to stimulate second language use and acquisition. One of the best sources in the mathematics curriculum for such enrichment activities is problem solving, specifically solving word problems. Furthermore, word problems, by virtue of their "language format," are a natural choice for language practice.

ESL teachers can develop sets of activities using word problems selected to fit various themes or instructional objectives. For example, lessons for elementary-level students can be built around word problems that give students practice with mathematics skills such as:

• each of the four basic operations—addition, subtraction, multiplication and division;

• basic operations with fractions and mixed numbers;

• basic operations with decimals;

• applying the concept of inverse operations; or

• estimating/rounding off the answer.

Lessons can also be built around specific language skills such as:

• learning sets of vocabulary that often designate the solution operation in word problems, both mathematics terms and natural-language words (e.g., *take away, decreased, have left,* and *lost* are some used with subtraction);

• learning sets of vocabulary that indicate comparisons (e.g., *fewer/more than, less/greater than*);

• learning how to read and understand problems written as hypothetical situations (i.e., practicing how to read and write *if* clauses);

• learning how to read and understand problems when the question is at the end, the beginning, or somewhere else in the problem; or practicing English composition skills through rewriting problems using different time references, changing singulars to plurals; or, at a more advanced level, writing paraphrases of the problems.

ESL teachers can simplify the job of finding word problems with the particular mathematics and/or language "specifications" they need for each activity by keeping a running file of problems on index cards. Word problems can be collected from mathematics texts, newspaper ads, and so on, or teachers and students can write them themselves. Suggestions follow for language-based activities using word problems.

Activity #1: Practice special mathematics vocabulary.

Materials needed: Food containers, or any other group of items for a "store."

Procedure: Set up a store with as many items as possible, each with a price clearly marked on it. The grocery store is always a good choice. Develop questions that refer to these marked items using terms such as *more than, less than, as much as, most, least, equal to, as many as, all together, twice as much as, fewer than, greater than, add, subtract,* and so on.

Sample questions based on a grocery store situation:

Name one item that costs more than $0.25 each.
How many apples can you buy with $0.50?

What costs more at this store, 3 apples or 3 oranges?

Activity #2: Problem Puzzles—Read all of the pieces of the problem and then put them in the order needed to make a "good" problem.

Materials needed: Word problem file, index cards or sentence strip, markers or pens.

Procedures: Select problems from your word problem file. Use any criteria you wish according to your activity objective. Type each piece of information (usually in elementary school, this means each sentence) on a strip of paper. (For primary grades, you may want to use sentence strips.) Identify each part of a problem with a number. Ask students to put the parts of the problem in order. You can make this as hard or as easy as you wish by varying the number of problems you mix up or put into the pool of pieces. You can also make this self-correcting by putting the correct puzzle number on the back of each strip.

Activity #3: Read the problem and tell whether there is too little, too much, or enough information to solve it.

Materials needed: A set of word problems with preferably the same number each of problems with too much information, not enough, and exactly enough. These can be put on a work sheet, on the board, or on index cards.

Procedures: From a group of word problem cards, have students read the problem and decide whether there is enough information to solve the problem, not enough, or too much. This activity can (and should) have a second or third step: If the problem has enough information, solve it; if the problem does not have enough information, add information that makes sense and solve the problem; if there is too much information, take out (or cross out) the extra information and then solve the problem. Since the exercise may be time-consuming, you may want to start with just one group of these problems such as those with too much information and work up to doing a group of mixed problems.

Samples:

THIS PROBLEM CONTAINS ENOUGH INFORMATION:

Margo bought 7 books last week. This week she bought three times as many books. How many books did she buy this week?

THIS PROBLEM HAS TOO MUCH INFORMATION:

138 fifth-graders are going on a trip to the zoo. They will take 3 buses. 72 of the students are boys and 66 are girls. There must be an equal number of students on each bus. How many students will ride on each bus?

THIS PROBLEM HAS NOT ENOUGH INFORMATION:

Peter bought 3 pounds of meat at $1.39 a pound. How much change did he receive?

Activity #4: Read the problem and fill in the missing information.

Materials needed: Sets of word problems, index cards or sentence strips, or dittos.

Procedure: Select a variety of problems (or select one particular set of problems). Go through these problems and leave out key words, phrases, whole pieces of information (i.e., sentences), the problem question. Make sure the problem is rewritten with plenty of space for the left-out portion. Have students fill in the blanks with whatever they think will make sense in the problem. To check whether students' "fill-ins" make sense, let the students try to solve the problem after the information is added.

Sample:

These problems omit some information:

> There were 2 basketball teams. How many children were on each team?

> Alfred bought 4 models for $1.75 each. How much change should he receive?

This problem omits the question:

> Mrs. Nguyen bought 3 cassette tapes for $7.98 each, including tax. She gave the clerk $30.00.

Activity # 5: Write a word problem from a word problem outline.

Materials needed: Word problem cards with the problem outline and paper and pencils (if for a written exercise).

Procedure: Write word problems based on problem outlines. You can use the outline format used in many mathematics texts in which just the bare, base phrases of information are given. Or you can make up your own outlines according to the kinds or problems you wish to practice or the language you would like to use.

Sample:

Problem outline:

9 tables
9 people at each table.
How many people in all?

Word problem written from the outline:

There were 9 tables in the school lunchroom. Nine people sat at each table. How many people in all were sitting at the lunchroom tables?

Activity 6: Write a word problem from a number sentence.

Materials needed: Index cards with the number sentence sets, or a blackboard. Use paper and pencil or a worksheet format if students are writing the problems.

Procedure: Select sets of number sentences. This activity works best if "families" of number sentences are used—those indicating inverse operations. For example, 3 x 4 = ?, 3 x ? = 12, 12 divided by 4 = ?, ? divided by 3 = 4, etc. Have students select a situation for each number sentence set and then have them make up a problem to fit each number sentence. The problem "fits" the number sentence if the number sentence is the one you use to solve the problem.

Sample:

Number sentence:

6 x 4 = [ ]

6 x [ ] = 24

Corresponding word problem:

Alex has 4 friends. He wants to buy each friend 6 cookies. How many cookies does Alex need to buy in all?

Alex has 24 cookies. He wants to divide the cookies evenly among his 4 friends. How many cookies will he give to each friend?

The word problem activities offered here are best used with small groups of three or four students. ESL teachers can organize their classes into groups according to students' language proficiency or mathematics background. In this way, problems can be selected to fit the ability of each group in order to keep interest levels high and frustration levels low. Teachers can also place more proficient students (in English or mathematics) in the problem-solving groups to act as tutors for their peers. However the groups are arranged, it is often best to start with problems that require easy mathematical solutions so that students can concentrate on the language of the problem while they get used to the process of problem solving (which is often new to them).

The advantage of using word problem activities in the manner described here is that they can be incorporated easily into most ESL curricula. Word problem activities can be built around almost any theme or instructional objective the ESL teacher might need to teach. The time spent on the activities can vary from a regular period each week covering many problems to 10 or 15 minutes per day or per week to work on one specific problem. Most important, time spent doing word problems is never wasted, even if students do not get around to actually solving the problems until later. From the mathematics point of view, LEP students can gain experience in doing different types of word problems in English and consequently become familiar with the general processes required for any kind of problem solving. At the same time, they are provided with numerous opportunities to use their second language for basic communication and communicating meaning in mathematics.

Closing Remarks

This chapter has provided mathematics and ESL educators with background information and instructional strategies that address the educational needs of LEP students. To this end, a brief overview of the nature of the language used in mathematics was given, as well as the role language plays in mathematics teaching and learning. On the basis of this information, suggestions for the adaptation or development of instructional strategies that integrate mathematics and second language learning in the mathematics and ESL classroom were illustrated. The underlying goal has been to assist teachers in the communication of mathematical content to students in order to develop mathematical and second language skills.

2
ESL
and Science Learning

Carolyn Kessler and Mary Ellen Quinn

> After a few minutes the sow bug die because it is
> hot to them and when they die they look like a
> circle. Putting the sow bug in the projector
> microscope and it is see big. They have hairs in
> the legs they look like tires in the back. The sow
> bug look like a armadillo.
>
> (*Mother Nature's Tiny Wonders,* 1984, p. 26)

Francisco, a Hispanic child of migrant workers in
rural Texas, wrote these results from observations
made while looking at a sow bug under an overhead
projector microscope during his fifth-grade science
class. Like all of his classmates, he had entered the fifth
grade in the fall unable to read or write English. His
home language was a nonstandard variety of Spanish,
and English was his second language. During his
previous years at school he had acquired an adequate
level of English proficiency for carrying out social
interactions with his teachers and peers. Academically,
however, his competence in English was extremely
limited. Scores on a standardized reading test indicated
that he was functioning at the first-grade level. The best
student in the class read at the second-grade level;
others were at a preprimer stage. Schooling for these
students, up to the start of fifth grade, had brought no
success and very limited English-language proficiency
for school purposes.

A sensitive fifth-grade teacher who understood the

cultural setting of his students, their level of cognitive development, their language needs, and the negative effects of prior school experiences challenged Francisco and his classmates to become readers and writers of English before the end of the school year. Using the content of science together with that of mathematics and social studies, Francisco and the other fifth-graders made an average gain of more than 3 years in reading levels and developed considerable enthusiasm for writing in English, their second language. The excitement of learning about culturally relevant sow bugs and armadillos in rural Texas became apparent. More important for long-range gains, however, was the fact that these children had developed English-language proficiency for academic purposes to the extent that they could know school success. Specifically, among other aspects of schooling, they had discovered the wonder of science inquiry and, simultaneously, had developed English competence needed for engaging in this inquiry (Hayes & Bahruth, 1985; Hayes, Bahruth, & Kessler, 1985). A process-oriented science class using an inquiry approach is among the optimal sources of social interaction and language input for facilitating acquisition of a second language (Kessler & Quinn, 1984; Mohan, 1986; Rodriguez & Bethel, 1983).

This chapter explores relationships between learning science and acquiring English as a second language (ESL) in relevant sociocultural contexts. Specifically, it considers ways in which science helps students with limited English proficiency (LEP) to develop in all aspects of language use at school: listening, speaking, reading, and writing.

Science Processes and Language

Science is generally defined as a set of concepts and relationships developed through the processes of observation, identification, description, experimental investigation, and theoretical explanation of natural phenomena.

Approaches to Science

When science is taught from an inquiry-based, problem-solving orientation, students learn to define a science problem, state a hypothesis, gather data, analyze data, and make statements relating the hypothesis to the data. Through scientific inquiry, students develop learning processes inherent in thinking: observing, classifying, comparing, communicating, measuring, inferring, predicting, and finding space and time relationships. These thinking processes, applied in a problem-solving format, lead to the development of the concepts of science.

A distinction between an inquiry approch to science education and a textbook-oriented approach is critical in any examination of the role of science in second language development. Emphasis on inquiry leads students to learn more about the "how" of science than the "what" and to understand that science is not a static body of knowledge but a dynamic quest. Overdependence on textbooks reduces the science class to exercises in literacy and develops a fundamental misunderstanding of the nature of science. For second language learners, dependence on textbooks in preference to hands-on investigation seriously constrains the conditions that facilitate language development. If students cannot understand the language of the textbook and have little or no opportunity to interact with others to gain meaning, their second language proficiency will not improve.

A lab-based inquiry approach to science must also be distinguished from science programs that rely largely on demonstrations by the teacher, promoting inquiry processes and language interactions only to a very limited extent. Science holds a unique position in the school curriculum in that it is one of the few content areas that emphasizes hands-on experimentation. An important dimension of science instruction is recognition of the learner's cognitive characteristics and how they interact with particular strategies to determine the overall effectiveness of instructional programs. Current science inquiry programs stress the cognitive processes of observing, inferring, predicting, hypothesizing, and experimenting. These and similar programs provide a rich environment for simultaneous cognitive and linguistic development. Confronted with observable natural events that set up a disequilibrium or cognitive conflict, in the Piagetian sense, children work hard to resolve the conflict if given the time to investigate and the opportunity to discuss their work.

In problem-solving, students must select and order varied types of data, using concepts that they already know to guide their search for answers to questions. This process leads to an understanding of new concepts and their relationships. Associated with this process are the efforts students make to convert these experiences to language. Francisco, in his lab report on observations about a sow bug, saw relationships between the bug's physical appearances and other phenomena in his world. He saw that a dead sow bug looked like a circle and that the hairs on its legs together with its shape made it look like a tire or even an armadillo.

The Language of Science

In a science textbook, abstract ideas are logically developed and linked through a number of linguistic devices: repetition of key words, use of paraphrase or semantically similar terms, and use of logical connectors such as *because, however, consequently*, and *for example*. These connectors indicate the nature of the relationship between the parts of a text. They can carry out a number of semantic functions. Science texts typically include connectors that signal addition or similarity, contradiction, cause and effect or reason and result, and chronological or logical sequence (Celce-Murcia & Larsen-Freeman, 1983). Although little research has been done to identify the difficulties that logical connectors present to ESL students in the context of science learning, a study of 16,530 students enrolled in grades 7-10 in Australia showed that substantial numbers of students experience difficulty with connectives used in various types of logial reasoning (Gardner, 1980). Other logical connectors in the language of science may be expected to pose particular problems for ESL students.

As children pass through the Piagetian stages of intellectual development, they learn first to make discoveries through sensorimotor activity, then to ask questions of adults, and finally to ask questions of themselves. An important component of science instruction, especially with older learners, aims to promote activities in which students are actively engaged in discussion with one another over the truth of hypotheses presented and the meaning of data gathered. The ability to ask questions, generate tentative answers, make predictions, and then evaluate evidence as supporting or rejecting the answers develops as a result of attempting to carry on discussions with others.

Students gradually internalize the linguistic elements necessary for hypothesis-testing and argumentation. Such internalization appears to be a prerequisite for aspects of proportional reasoning and other types of advanced reasoning used in science. The ability, for example, to raise questions about a problem, generate hypotheses, make predictions, and design an experiment to test the hypotheses rests on the gradual internalization of the linguistic elements involved (A. Lawson, D.I. Lawson, & C.A. Lawson, 1984). To the extent that science students do not have access to these linguistic abilities, they cannot successfully engage in science inquiry that demands this kind of reasoning. Thus, ESL students who do not yet have the necessary linguistic elements in their first language or who are unfamiliar with their use in the second language may be expected to have particular difficulty in science reasoning.

In a study of factors affecting academic achievement in a second language, Saville-Troike (1984) found that knowledge of vocabulary is the most important aspect of second language competence for learning academic content through that language. Knowledge of vocabulary is more important than knowledge of English morphology such as plural markers on nouns or past tense markers on verbs, and even knowledge of syntactic structures for sentence patterns. Furthermore, it is one thing to be able to use language socially, and another to use it academically. Linguistically, the most important aspect of language the ESL student needs is vocabulary.

Specialized vocabulary is closely tied to the specific content of science. In a study of science textbooks that are widely used in grades 6 through 9, Hurd, Robinson, McConnell, and Ross (1981) found that more than 2,500 new words were introduced each year. They point out that this figure is twice what is commonly expected in a foreign language class of the same grade level. Terminology, nevertheless, is a central feature of the textbooks that most science classes use as major determiners of what students must do and learn in science (Yager, 1983). While the heightened importance of terminology is a general problem of science education, the abundance of new terms poses particular problems for ESL learners. Recognition of such problems is crucial in light of the growing evidence that knowledge of vocabulary is essential to learning academic content through a second language.

Students' ability to recognize scientific concept definitions and their verbal labels is a feature of science communication. Lynch, Chipman, and Pachaury (1985) studied a set of key concept words used in defining the nature of matter (e.g., atom, solid, element). In administering equivalent tests to 10th-graders in Australia, using English, and in India, using Hindi, they found identical scores for both groups. Item analysis of the test, however, showed considerable variations in the order of recognition for specific terms. In one paradigm dealing with spatial and relational notions, for example, the order for English speakers was area before mass; for Hindi students the corresponding order was mass before area. In another paradigm on the physical form of matter, English students scored consistently higher on the set of terms about the states of matter (i.e., solid, liquid, gas). Hindi students, on the other hand, showed higher socres for terms dealing with the substructure of the atom (i.e., electron, proton, neutron). Differences in the order of development for science vocabulary are attributed, at least in part, to linguistic and cultural variables in the home languages. Findings such as these have implications for teaching science in ESL. Differences in first language and culture may play a role in the development of scientific language to an extent that is generally overlooked.

The language of science is complex, and much has

yet to be analyzed in its relationship to the needs of the ESL student studying science. However, several basic principles should be kept in mind when working with the LEP student:

1. Students' acquisition of new terminology or new structures requires the presentation of these items in science contexts, not in lists of isolated items;

2. The more students are physically engaged in hands-on activities that involve talking about concepts, the sooner the language of science will be acquired;

3. Simultaneously, language in general will develop from the communicative context in which it is used (Mohan, 1986).

Fortunately, much of the terminology and symbol system used in science is recognized internationally, a facilitating factor for the older ESL student with prior science instruction in his or her first language. Nevertheless, the development of the language of science, or the scientific register, is a major consideration in using science content with ESL students.

Ethnoscience and Language

Culture, as a term in social science, refers to learned and shared standards for ways of thinking, feeling, and acting (Erickson, 1986). Teaching science across cultures requires taking into account cultural differences and considering how they affect concept development.

All cultures have well-developed theories about how the physical world operates without studying formal science. Even young children before beginning instruction in science have knowledge that they use to explain and make predictions about their physical world. *Ethnoscience* refers to theories and procedures for learning about the physical world that have evolved informally within cultures to explain and predict natural phenomena. Children, through membership in

a cultural group and through constraints of development, bring their theories of ethnoscience to the study of
formal science in the school setting. These folk or naive
theories provide culturally satisfactory explanations
and predictions and by and large permit successful
functioning in the physical world. They are, however,
difficult to replace or modify in formal science instruction (Champagne, 1986).

One major difference between formal science and
ethnoscience is in the meaning of terms. An example is
in use of the terms *velocity* and *acceleration*. From the
standpoint of ethnoscience, these terms are synony-
mous. In formal science they are rigorously distinguished: *velocity* is the rate of change of position,
acceleration is the rate of change of velocity. Even after
formal science instruction, however, many individuals
continue to confuse these terms in talking about forward motion. A further illustration of persistent beliefs
about motion is commonly found in accounts of what
happens to a ball dropped by a person who is running.
In spite of formal science study, many remain con-
vinced that the ball falls straight down, failing to adopt
the basic principle that the ball will continue to move in
a forward as well as downward motion (McCloskey,
1983).

Ethnoscientific theories are generally applicable to a
much narrower range of natural phenomena than
those of formal science. Formal science, for example,
has one theory to explain both the motion of a ball in free
fall and that of one rolling down an inclined plane.
Ethnoscience may have two separate theories to explain
motion in these different settings.

In another example of ethnoscience, M. Smith (1986)
points out that Native American Cree and Objibway
people traditionally classify plants and animals according to their function and use. Formal science classifies
them according to structure. While children univer-
sally carry out the process of classification, the system
of classification made available to them is arbitrary.
The classification systems of ethnoscience and formal
science in this case are both valid, just different.

Ethnoscientific perspectives can influence all of the
thinking activities of science—from observation and

classification to inference and prediction. Although formal science typically presents concepts as if all students conceptualize their physical environment in the same way and ethnoscience recognizes that students from diverse cultural backgrounds may, in fact, differ in science-related thinking processes, the exact nature and extent of these differences is not fully understood. In a study of spatial thinking processes for Navajo 6th- and 10th-grade students, H.G. Cohen (1985) found no substantial differences in the development of selected spatial abilities for American Indian children living in the traditional culture of the reservation when compared with non-American Indian students.

The extent to which science programs should be redesigned to make them ethnically relevant is a matter of debate. For ESL and science teachers, however, the principle remains that all children share a set of universal thinking abilities, regardless of first language or culture. At the same time, teachers must be aware that cultural differences may frame the view of the world differently for LEP students. The learner's ethnoscientific theories provide the starting point for science instruction and, consequently, for the ESL student's language development in science contexts. The ESL teacher and the science teacher both enter into the complex role of bridging cross-cultural differences and mediating intercultural understanding.

Science and ESL teachers who fail to take into account ethnoscienctific viewpoints, both culture- and age-related, can easily misinterpret the LEP student's ability to understand the language of science instruction. Although the surface form of the language may be understood, the underlying cognitive restructuring needed to change a naive theory may not have occurred. Communication breakdowns may arise, then, not from language but from conceptual notions about the physical world. The necessary cognitive change may not take place unless or until students experience a sociocognitive conflict. Such a conflict is triggered by a combination of social interaction and the use of manipulative materials for observing physical events.

Sociocognitive conflict also facilitates the acquisition of a second language. Engaging LEP children in social interaction not only creates internal conflict for re-structuring ways of thinking about the physical world, but also provides the language environment needed for linguistic development.

Language Acquisition Processes in Science Contexts

"Doing science" is a risk-taking activity. Experi-menting with physical realities does not offer preset, error-proof outcomes. It often involves many false starts, modifications, restatements, and the need to gather more data as input for reformulating hypoth-eses. Likewise, "doing language," or acquiring a new linguistic system, is a risk-taking activity. Experiment-ing with linguistic elements does not guarantee suc-cessful communication. Negotiating meaning during interactions, oral or written, also involves false starts, editing, paraphrases or restatements, and the need for more input to reorganize or reformulate hypotheses about the developing language system. Risk-taking, in science inquiry or language use, involves hypothesis-testing processes. Such processes necessarily hold ele-ments of uncertainty and the possibility of error or failure. The science student makes guesses about physical outcomes; the language student makes them about communicative outcomes. For language learners, guesses apply both to meaning, or what is said, and to form, or how it is said.

As Beebe (1983) observes, nearly all of the attempts to use a new language productively are risk-taking acts. Successful language learners are willing to take these risks in spite of possible negative consequences. Fran-cisco, for example, took risks in writing his science lab report. He made many errors in form, including omis-sion of required past tense markers, incorrect preposi-tions, pronouns marked for wrong number, an incor-rect article, errors in the verb phrase, omission of a sentence subject. For Francisco, the consequences were positive. The teacher praised his efforts and understood his intended meaning. Efforts such as these gradually facilitated the development of English as he moved from the virtual absence of academic competence in English at the beginning of the year to a level at which he functioned with considerable success.

Acquiring a second language is a sociocognitive process resulting from efforts to take part in communicative interactions. As the exchange and negotiation of conceptual, sociocultural, and affective content, science provides a form of social interaction that qualifies as genuine language use and thus a context for language acquisition. Defining language acquisition as a natural, subconscious process that takes place when the focus is on communication or meaning, Krashen (1982) argues that this process is central to second language development. The amount and quality of language that the student receives and understands are critical factors in determining language proficiency outcomes.

Science meets requirements for an optimal source of relevant, comprehensible language input, affectively positive conditions of high interest and low anxiety, and opportunities to engage in genuine communicative interaction. Tapping the thinking processes associated with science sets conditions for the simultaneous development of scientific concepts and language. In summary, the interaction between science and ESL development is threefold:

- providing language input to engage thinking processes;
- facilitating positive affective variables; and
- structuring group interactions in an academic setting.

Language Input

Science offers a particularly rich source of input for the ESL learner. For elementary school students such as Francisco, it provides experience in the elements of scientific concepts and basics in the language of science. The same could also be said for the secondary school and college or university science student; the overall principles are not age-dependent. Extensive use of graphics, definitions of new terms, use of fairly simple syntactic structures, and explicit and easy-to-understand directions for carrying out investigations all contribute to the transmission of meanings. Input such as this corresponds closely to Krashen's (1982) view of optimal input—comprehensible, meaningful, and relevant. Pictures, diagrams, graphs, and other visuals typically found in science texts and laboratory manuals supply extralinguistic contexts for helping LEP students grasp the intended meaning. Vocabulary, new to native speakers as well as ESL students, is often given with a bold-faced definition or a visual. This contributes to clarifying meaning and provides opportunities for the acquisition of terms and related language forms. Effective science instruction draws extensively on a variety of devices, linguistic and extralinguistic, to ensure comprehension.

Science, in many ways, helps the ESL learner get the input necessary for language acquisition. To the older student with prior science instruction, the basic types of scientific discourse may already be familiar: descriptions, reports, instructions for laboratory procedures, accounts of experiments, and statements of conclusions and generalizations. Recognition of these discourse forms in a new language draws on basic scientific reasoning processes and helps to make the new language input understood. For younger students not yet familiar with these discourse uses of language, science texts and laboratory manuals present new meanings in clear, comprehensible language.

In addition to the science teacher, the texts, and the laboratory manuals, the interaction of the ESL student with peers also serves to generate input. Interactions during science investigations call for a wide range of language functions, including requesting, informing, seeking clarifications, and making observations. Following directions, carrying out investigative procedures, observing results, and drawing conclusions constitute aspects of the genuine use of language found in science. Language used in science contexts such as these provides a rich source of input for the ESL learner. The oral language used in science experiences and the literacy demands in reading textual material, following procedures for conducting investigations, and writing follow-up reports contribute to the overall development of ESL.

Affective Variables

High interest and motivation, intrinsic to scientific inquiry, are major contributors to second language development. Affective variables such as motivation, self-confidence, and anxiety promote or hinder the mental processes governing language development. An effective language development environment provides comprehensible input in a low-anxiety setting. Science meets these requirements.

When students are actively engaged in science, the focus is on the physical events taking place. Language use revolves around relating observations or communicating other aspects of the investigation. Because students are focusing on *what* is being said–meaning –they are not paying explicit attention to *how* messages are expressed–their form. Errors in language form are passed over as long as they do not disrupt communication. If understanding does break down, various strategies may be used to determine the meaning and continue the activity. Looking puzzled, asking what a word means, and repeating a sentence or phrase with a question intonation are various strategies learners use to cope with not understanding. Such coping mechanisms, often referred to as *strategic competence,* are used in abundance by good language learners. In a supportive classroom setting, use of such strategies does not cause learners to become overanxious or feel threatened. Because science experiences are intrinsically interesting, language learners readily use these strategies while maintaining positive attitudes and continuing to receive the input needed for language development.

Affective variables play a critical role in second language development for learners of all ages. Attitudes toward the new language and culture may intersect with the affective climate set in the classroom. Negative responses in any of these dimensions can inhibit second language development, just as very positive ones can promote it (Fillmore, 1979).

A major role of the teacher, science or ESL, is to make certain that students understand intended meanings. The teacher also keeps anxiety levels lowered by not demanding language production prematurely or requiring error-free production when students try to use the language. Correction is focused on the truth value of the language used in terms of scientific accuracy, interpretation, analysis, creativity, and evaluation. Many errors in form are naturally eradicated as the learner develops more of the language system. Errors in written activities, including lab reports, may be addressed through nonthreatening techniques such as those used in teaching writing, including peer editing and teacher conferencing (Calkins, 1986).

Learner Interactions and Classroom Structure

The classroom structure, which includes instructional style and student composition, can inhibit or promote second language acquisition.

In a longitudinal study of young children acquiring English as a second language, Fillmore (1983) found that a relatively open class structure works only if enough native English speakers are in the class to enable sustained interactions with the ESL learners. In an open, interactive setting, the amount of language input to any individual student depends on the student's own ability to seek out others in the class who speak English and to initiate some kind of meaningful exchange with them. Because of each learner's unique set of personality characteristics, not all students can do this equally well. For classrooms with a high concentration of second language learners, a more teacher-centered approach may be necessary, particularly if the ESL students share the same first language. The teacher must then structure and manage the activities in such a way as to ensure that each student has adequate access to second language input.

Science presents extensive opportunities for student interaction. Laboratory work is a type of open classroom that provides enough structure and management to make conditions for second language development possible even when the concentration of ESL students is high.

Science labs normally require students to work together in small groups. ESL learners doing science investigations together receive language input and participate in meaningful negotiations. Even when the interaction is between nonnative speakers of English, the quantity and variety of language practice and the quality of the process for arriving at an understanding of meaning through group work continue to facilitate second language acquisition (Long & Porter, 1985).

Science labs also provide language learners helpful variations for getting input. Students often have opportunities in a lab to act as peer tutors. In a study with Mexican-American LEP and monolingual English-speaking students, Johnson (1983) found that structured peer-tutoring sessions focused on the natural use of English led to significant increases in vocabulary for the LEP children. In carefully structured settings designed for exchanges of information in English, LEP students functioned as tutors for the non-LEP students in this study. Science labs provide a similar structure in the sense that the role of tutor may alternate within the group. The ESL student may at times be a tutor as the group completes all the steps necessary for the lab, and at other times be the one tutored. Benefits are derived in either case.

Peer interaction must also take into account factors that can potentially alter its effectiveness. As Cohen and Anthony (1982) explain in detail, classroom social status affects the frequency of student interaction. Interaction itself affects the amount of learning. They found that children with higher social status have more access to interaction and that children not fully proficient in English are perceived as having lower status. For peer interaction to be effective, status effects must be treated. One program that has reported effective results in modifying status effects is the Finding Out/Descubrimiento curriculum developed by De Avila and Duncan (1984). This bilingual science/mathematics program makes use of learning centers in which children take turns at various assigned roles. They gradually understand that new learning draws on not just a single ability but a number of unrelated ones. This multiple-ability approach to peer interaction reduces negative status effects, allowing all students to experience the significant learning gains from group interactions. Students learn to use one another as resources regardless of linguistic differences. Interaction in this type of heterogeneous grouping facilitates conceptual learning for all students. When classrooms are organized so that LEP students have access to interactive settings, students can acquire both science and English simultaneously (De Avila, 1983).

Cognitive Benefits

For children developing a second language at school, access to two languages appears to have positive effects on cognitive functioning once students reach a certain threshold level of bilingual linguistic competence (Cummins, 1976). Studies from a wide range of sociocultural contexts indicate that children who know two languages may have an advantage over monolinguals on various measures of cognitive abilities, consistent with Cummins' hypothesis. Positive effects appear even before the second language learner has fully balanced proficiency in two languages.

In a science education program comparing monolingual English-speaking sixth-grade children with bilingual peers using ESL, Kessler and Quinn (1982, 1985) found that bilinguals performed significantly better than monolinguals in formulating solutions to science problems. For this study, physical science problems were presented through 3-minute film loops. Students then collected data by asking yes/no questions of the teacher. The film session ended with students writing as many hypotheses as possible in a rigorously controlled 12-minute period. In discussion sessions following presentation of the film loops and the writing of hypotheses, children learned how to judge their own hypotheses and how to make use of their observations and inferences to generate hypotheses of higher quality. The ability to generate multiple solutions to a problem illustrates an aspect of divergent thinking. In addition, children using ESL were superior in convergent thinking, as seen in the linguistic process of metaphor formation (Quinn & Kessler, 1986). The similes in Francisco's lab report relating sow bugs, circles, tires, and armadillos give evidence of this process. Research on the interaction of cognition and language with science suggests that bilingual children may enter into divergent and convergent thinking more fully than their monolingual peers.

Drawing on interaction between cognitive structures and cultural experiences, science provides the external events to challenge existing cognitive systems by presenting inconsistencies to existing systems. Efforts to use two languages can also function as a source of disequilibrium because competing linguistic codes are available to the learner. This conflict leads bilingual individuals to build new cognitive systems at higher levels. Affective disequilibrium triggers the feeling that "something is wrong" or that "it doesn't fit" and contributes to the process. For bilingual children, even those not fully proficient in the second language, efforts to "make things fit" cognitively, affectively, and linguistically in science problem-solving engage brain mechanisms that stimulate both language and cognitive development. This interaction facilitates positive gains linguistically and cognitively for all children, but possibly more fully for dual-language users (Kessler & Quinn, 1982).

In a study of 64 Mexican-American LEP third-graders, Rodriguez and Bethel (1983) found that science inquiry facilitated the development of classification skills and English oral language communication simultaneously. In a series of 30 science lessons that introduced scientific concepts by requiring the manipulation of concrete objects such as rocks, buttons, blocks, and shells, children learned to make observations, comparisons, and descriptions. They eventually learned to group objects on the basis of perceived and inferred attributes. Each lesson introduced specific terms appropriate to the objects, such as solubility, texture, and permeability. In developing the language of science, children learned new vocabulary in context, word meanings, and operational definitions of terms. They learned how to use the precise and descriptive language of science. Manipulating and classifying objects gave children opportunities to talk about something they were doing. Interactions with peers and the teacher were an important part of carrying out the classification tasks. Having something new, different, and interesting to talk about contributed to oral language development in ESL. As a result of the science lessons, scores improved significantly on a test of classification skills and on a test measuring oral language skills. The inquiry approach used in this study specifically identifies contributions of the following to the successful simultaneous development of cognitive and linguistic processes in a science context:

- use of manipulative materials;
- teacher's interaction with the children;
- peer interaction;
- independent work; and
- discovery of relationships through activity.

The Finding Out/Descubrimiento curriculum mentioned earlier (De Avila & Duncan, 1984) is a bilingual science and mathematics program that has been effectively implemented in a number of schools with Spanish-dominant children acquiring English. Designed for use with small groups, the 130 activities are divided into 17 units covering principles of physics and mathematics in a way that relates them to children's interests and experience. By structuring activities to encourage collaborative problem-solving, the program is directed toward development of higher-level cognitive skills. At the same time, activities also make use of both oral and written language in Spanish and English. Through concrete experimentation and interaction with the teacher and peers, students are actively involved in completing their tasks as they talk and work together.

A project using the Finding Out materials with more than 300 children in nine bilingual classrooms in San Jose, Calif., grades two through four, indicates a number of gains (De Avila, 1983; De Avila, Cohen, & Intili, 1981). The linguistically heterogeneous sample included monolingual Spanish-speaking and English-speaking children together with others at various levels of bilingual proficiency in Spanish and English. Results from the Multicultural Improvement of Cognitive Abilities (MICA) project show that participants made improvements not only in cognitive and academic achievements but also in language proficiency. Success is attributed to factors including a classroom organization encouraging students to talk with each other while doing intellectually challenging activities and the availability of a wide variety of linguistic subgroups. For LEP children, the availability of peers who can provide English language input is an important resource. Language proficiency gains are a by-product of problem-solving interactions in linguistically heterogeneous groups such as those of the MICA project. The positive effects of one group on the other argues for not dividing a class into separate linguistic subgroups for instructional purposes.

A typical activity for the Finding Out curriculum is the following activity taken from the unit on electricity (De Avila & Duncan, 1984). The teacher's guide and all materials are given in both Spanish and English. For purposes of illustration, the English portion is provided here.

Title: **CONNECT A BULB**

Purpose: **To investigate circuits**

Materials: Variety of cell batteries, insulated wire (with 3 cm of insulation removed at ends), flashlight bulbs, pencils, worksheets

Corresponding Operations (Concepts):

Inference: predicting which bulbs will light on the basis of prior experience with batteries and bulbs

Multiple classes/inclusion-exclusion: identifying working and nonworking ways to connect batteries and bulbs

Inference: understanding why some arrangements work, some don't; grasping concept of circuitry

(Students working in small groups complete a worksheet to show the ways to connect circuits that will work. They are asked to draw circuits that work in the box on the left-hand side of the page and those that do not in the box on the right-hand side.)

Suggestions for Teacher-Student Interactions:

1. What did you think about when you made your predictions?

2. What did you notice about all the ones that worked? How about the ones that did not work?

3. In what other ways do we use circuits? House, school, towns, phones . . . ?

Vocabulary: **connect, battery, bulb, wire, predict, circuit**

The teacher's role is one of facilitator and manager, asking appropriate questions and guiding the children's experiences as they work in small groups, pairs, or even individually at the learning centers. ESL development takes place naturally as LEP children do the activities that emphasize how children think through a given problem.

Science Learning and Second Language Acquisition

Evidence indicates that ESL students can simultaneously develop new science concepts and acquire a new language. As De Avila (1983) points out, LEP students will develop science concepts as readily as mainstream students while they acquire English proficiency provided that certain conditions are met. This point is critical because it argues against models of language and science instruction that require certain levels of linguistic proficiency before the introduction of new scientific concepts. Such models may use science for language development but tap basic, prior science knowledge as a source of input for language acquisition, dealing with new scientific concepts in the student's first language before introducing them in the second language (Penfield & Ornstein-Galicia, 1981).

In conceptualizing an Integrative Language Development Approach as a counter-model in which both language proficiency and academic content can develop together, Milk (1985) identifies two critical elements: integration of second language development into regular content-area instruction and creation of appropriate conditions for providing input. Success for this model, as Milk suggests, rests on cooperative learning in heterogeneous small-group settings. This entails:

• grouping strategies;
• alternate ways for providing input;
• techniques for making subject matter comprehensible; and
• opportunities to develop language proficiency for academic purposes.

Given the necessary conditions, the result is the development of cognitive/academic language proficiency (CALP), the literacy-related aspects of language use necessary for school success (Cummins, 1981, 1984).

Evidence suggests that LEP students can develop new scientific concepts in either bilingual or monolingual English environments. ESL is used in either case. When the conditions necessary for second language acquisition are present, English develops along with scientific concepts for LEP students.

ESL and Secondary School Science

Ho (1982) conducted a study of the relationship between physics achievement and the language of instruction with 10th-graders in Hong Kong. Chinese students who were taught physics in English, their second language, by a nonnative speaker of English learned the content of physics as well as peers who were instructed in Chinese, their native language. Achievement in physics was not impeded by using the second language as a medium of instruction. On an English proficiency test that assessed listening comprehension, English structure, vocabulary, reading comprehension, and writing ability, the mean percentile for the Chinese

ESL students was 54, an intermediate proficiency level.

A case study of the acquisition of ESL by a native speaker of Gujarati conducted by Kessler and Quinn (1984) provides evidence of substantial English-language development in the context of a physical science course. Data from lab reports show that during an academic year the student moved out of a beginning preproductive stage, systematically and extensively acquiring vocabulary, syntactic structures, and the mechanics of writing. Language development occurred without the teacher correcting language forms. Evaluations of work rested on the scientific accuracy of the reports. Data for the case study were 20 lab reports collected in a physical science class along with personal letters to the teacher in an ESL class during the course of the year. The science class and the ESL class were taught by the same teacher. Written data for the lab reports provide a source for analyzing the development of form-function relationships with emphasis on following written directions, identifying materials, describing procedures, making observations, stating hypotheses, and drawing conclusions. In addition to analysis of the linguistic system, students' handwriting and the mechanics of written English—spelling, punctuation, and capitalization—were examined to gain insight into acquisition of English literacy. Letters written in the ESL class corroborated language proficiency shown on the lab reports.

The students followed a format prescribed by the teacher for all science reports, giving:

- the title of the science experiment as stated in the text;
- the problem as synthesized by the student;
- the materials as listed in the directions;
- the procedure as summarized from the detailed version in the text;
- the presentation of findings or observations as determined by the actual lab experience; and
- the conclusions drawn from the data gathered.

With this format, lab reports typically generated language that in some parts was copied from the text and in others was produced creatively by the student. The following example of a report on the force of friction based on directions found in the science text (Bickel, Eigenfeld, & Hogg, 1973) represents the early stage of English development:

Title: The force of friction and the waight of a Body

Babelm: what happned to the force book.

Materials = spring scale; loop of thread; 4 Textbook

Procedure — Four textbook will be needed for this experiment, so should work in groups of four. Find the weight of book by means of a spiring scale, and record the weight

number of book	weight of Book in newton	force of (Friction) in newton
1	9 N	$3^{1}/_{2}$ N
2	18 N	$6^{1}/_{4}$ N
3	27 N	10 N
4	36 N	12 N

Congusenel — the book differce newten and twice time

The student clearly understood and followed the procedures in recording the weights and calculating the force of friction, arriving at a reasonably appropriate conclusion even though verbalization posed problems. Errors are present for both copying and productive language use, but the main meaning is conveyed.

During the year the student generated increasingly more productive language, and the quality of language used in writing lab reports showed marked changes. The following report on the solubility of sodium chloride shows the level of ESL development reached by the end of the year.

Titals= To Find the Solubility of Sodium Chloride by Evaporating a Saturated Solution

Problem: find solubility of sodium chloride

Materials= 100 ml graduate; evaporating dish; equal-arm balance; stand;
      4-inch ring, wire gauze; burner

procedure: 1) find the mass of the evaporating dish, pour the solution
               into the dish

            2) Attach the ring to the stand so that the ring is about 10
               cm above the top of the burner

            3) When the salt appears to be dry, heat the dish strongly
               with the full flam of the burner

data:
      1)   mass of empty dish   44.2 g
      2)   mass of dish plus solution   66
      3)   mass of solution   21.8 g
      4)   mass dish plus salt   51.4
      5)   mass of salt   7.2
      6)   mass of water   14.6
      7)   volume of water (ml)   14.6
      8)   solubility of NaCl   49.3

$$\frac{\text{mass of salt (g)}}{\text{volume of water (ml)}} \times 100$$

Congulsen: Salt is very solubility in water.

By this stage, the student paraphrases and sum-
marizes much more extensively than at the beginning
of the year, relying much less on copying from the text,
and fewer errors appear in language forms and writing
mechanics.

ESL and Elementary School Science

In Francisco's fifth-grade bilingual class in
Pearsall, Texas, science was an integral part of the
curriculum. Students, usually working with partners,
regularly designed their own investigations. On the
pattern of the high school physical science reports, they
also wrote up their investigations. Since all students in
the class were classified as LEP, science activities in
English were simultaneously ESL activities. A major
project of the year was to write, as a class, a series of

books, including two on science. Students wrote and edited their material, adding illustrations where appropriate. The teacher provided examples and served as a resource person, but did not correct the work before its publication.

A typical science report produced by late March of that year is the following on using an overhead projector microscope to study insects.

A flea

MATERIALS: one flea, paper, projector miscroscope, two glass slides

PROCEDURE:

1) Get a dog or a cat.
2) Then get the dog's ear and you can find a bunch of fleas.
3) Get the flea with your finger nails and pull it out.
4) Put it in a small bag about the size of a cigar bag.
5) Put the flea on a glass slide and then put the other glass slide on top.
6) Put the glass slide on the projector microsope.
7) Turn on the projector miscrosope.
8) Focus.

RESULTS:

First the flea was little and then the flea was big. And the flea had like a needle on front of his head. The flea had like hair on there feet and on there back. And the flea is fat but when it's out of focus it looks skinny and little. *(illustration given)*

Having started the year basically as nonreaders of English, these fifth-graders literally wrote their way to reading through this process (Hayes, Bahruth, & Kessler, 1985).

Research evidence from teaching science in English to LEP students indicates that both science and language can develop at the same time when conditions for effective science inquiry and second language acquisition are met through the classroom structure and management. This goal entails adjustments in the materials to meet language needs, extensive peer and teacher interactions, and intrinsically interesting and cognitively enriching activities for the ESL student.

Materials for Science and ESL Development

Materials designed specifically for the simultaneous development of scientific concepts and ESL are not yet widely available. In most cases, teachers are left with the task of trying to adapt texts and activities designed for native speakers of English. Knowing how to use the materials at hand, however, can lead to successful experiences for both science and language learning. The physical science investigations by a high school student, the examinations of the environment by migrant children, the classifications made by third-graders, the hypotheses formulated by sixth-graders, all discussed in this chapter, indicate that science and ESL can develop together even without uniquely prepared materials provided that they are used under appropriate conditions.

To help teachers make appropriate adaptations for science materials, many school districts have developed science curriculum guides that serve as a resource in working with LEP students. Written by classroom teachers in many cases, these guides typically give specific objectives for a lesson, identify relevant vocabulary, and present a set of activities to carry out the objectives. Following is an example of a lesson designed for use with kindergartners adapted from a science guide for the Northside Independent School District in San Antonio, Texas (Hayes & Pearce, 1985). It is intended for use with a wide range of English proficiency levels.

Physical Science Strand: ENERGY

Sample Activities:

1) Shake coffee cans and decide if the sound is loud or soft

2) Listen to a sound made by the teacher or leader with an unknown instrument out of sight of the children. Have students identify the object.

3) Listen to a rhythm clapped. Identify it as loud or soft. Reproduce the rhythm.

4) Make a telephone. See what will carry sound vibrations.

5) Make drums from empty coffee cans and oatmeal boxes. Compare the sounds and discuss why one is louder than the other.

6) Make a xylophone from jars to see and hear how vibrations are made.

For children acquiring English, these activities help to develop concepts associated with sounds along with relevant vocabulary presented in a meaningful experience. Manipulating objects such as cans or jars, acquiring data through the senses by listening to various kinds of sounds, classifying sounds into loud or soft, and developing the concept of sound vibration are all part of scientific inquiry. Communicating data by identifying objects and describing and contrasting sounds are activities that contribute to language development at the same time. Activities such as clapping to reproduce a rhythm or following the teacher's directions to make a telephone are similar to those of Total Physical Response, a methodology for second language teaching (Asher, 1982).

For older children who can read in their first language, supplementary materials for the science text may help develop language necessary to participate more fully in class activities and at the same time contribute to understanding of the science content. Kessler and Fathman (1985) developed one such set of materials to accompany a commercially available science series. Designed to help students get meaningful input from reading the science text and from interacting with the teacher and peers, the activities draw on a variety of cognitive and language activities.

The following exercise for the unit on electricity and magnetism for sixth grade illustrates how the text is integrated into the reading and writing activities (Kessler & Fathman, 1985, p. 35).

Unit: ELECTRICITY AND MAGNETISM

Exercise F: Read about conductors of electricity on pages 160 and 162 of your book. Decide if each of the following things is a good or a poor conductor of electricity. Write it in the correct box below.

aluminum   copper wire   paper
rubber balloon   eraser   gold
silver   plastic

GOOD CONDUCTORS   POOR CONDUCTORS

(box for list)   (box for list)

1. Why are some things good conductors of electricity?
2. How are poor conductors useful?

The items listed for classification are pictured and labeled either in the text itself or in the ESL workbook. Before this exercise, students have completed a number of others that contribute to the gradual buildup of the vocabulary associated with electric currents, circuits, and conductors. As they acquire vocabulary for these concepts they can engage in class inquiry built around these notions. In linguistically heterogeneous classes, peers can serve as tutors to help ESL learners successfully complete the exercises. The teacher, peers, textbook, and workbook all serve as sources of input for language acquisition in the context of science lessons.

At the secondary school level, a text by Fathman and Quinn (forthcoming) is designed to provide ESL or science teachers with a series of ideas specifically for teaching scientific concepts to LEP students. Organized around a unifying theme of energy, the text consists of a cohesive set of science discovery lessons together with suggested language exercises. All students participate in the investigations, but the teacher's explanations, vocabulary, and language exercises can be directed to the specific needs of students at varying English language proficiency levels. The language exercises follow a notional/functional approach, relating language functions with specific scientific concepts. Each chapter includes descriptions and directions for three kinds of activities: a teacher's demonstration, a group activity, and an individual activity. The teacher's demonstration gives students the opportunity to listen and observe before producing any language. For the group activity, students work together in setting up and

group activity, students work together in setting up and carrying out a simple investigation. Student interaction is encouraged through observing, recording, and interpreting the data obtained. For the individual activity, specific directions are given for what to use and what to do. Following each type of activity, suggestions are given for language exercise, including vocabulary, what to discuss (listening and speaking), and what to record (reading and writing). Worksheets accompany each of the physical or life science activities, providing exercises for ESL students at varying proficiency levels. Drawing on current approaches to both language and science teaching, the text is intended for use by ESL and science teachers working individually or as a team. It is designed for both experienced and inexperienced teachers to give assistance in teaching language while presenting content related to the science curriculum.

The following sample activity from the text is excerpted from the chapter on animals. The science concept for this chapter is to show that animals are living things that move from place to place on their own power. Related language functions emphasize making suggestions and expressing opinions. Science and language notes to the teacher are included to provide any necessary background in doing the activities. Science notes summarize the basic concepts around which the chapter is organized. Language notes give the linguistic background for the form and function relationships used in the science content.

Title: ANIMALS THAT MAKE TRACKS

Activity: Teacher demonstration

Topic: Observing how some animals make tracks when they move

What to Do: Listen to the teacher and follow directions as the teacher shows you how tracks are made.

Words to Study:

Beginning: animal, human, tracks, newspaper, clay, move, walk, print, across, sand, mud

Advanced: characteristic, energy of motion, pattern, a set, a series,

What to Discuss:

1) Make suggestions to your classmates on how to look for tracks in places outside of your classroom. For example, you might say, "Why don't you look in sand for tracks?" or "If I were you, I'd look in mud."

2) Suggest where you think the best tracks might be found.

3) Describe different track patterns.

4) Discuss the questions. What are some animals that make tracks? How are tracks made? What other things besides animals make tracks? What do tracks of different sizes and shapes tell us? Where are tracks often found? Why are tracks evidence of energy of motion?

What to Record:

1) Draw a picture of the tracks that some of the students made when they walked in the powder.

2) Write the names of animals that make tracks and the best place to find the tracks.

(Appropriate forms for making these recordings are given.)

Activities continue with a variety of language exercises. Among them are drawing circles around terms, identifying and writing the most polite suggestions in a set and writing answers to questions based on the investigation of animal tracks.

In subsequent activities, students work in small groups and, later, independently on further elaboration of the concepts involving the motion of animals and the language functions of suggesting and expressing opinions.

Whether designed for kindergarten, upper elementary, or secondary school students, the sample activities presented here are illustrative of how science and language development can take place together. It can occur under the direction of the ESL teacher or the science teacher. Successful implementation, however, rests on a number of factors. In addition to classroom structure and management and providing a climate for language interaction and input, a key factor is the ESL teacher's willingness to handle basic science concepts or the science teacher's sensitivity to basic notions of second language acquisition. For both, it is important to understand that the oral exchanges in the science classroom or laboratory contribute to the development of listening and speaking, or spoken discourse. Writing to learn science (Johnston, 1985) can develop literacy for both reading and writing. The written discourse found in texts, lab manuals, or student-generated material is crucial for the development of the ability to function academically in ESL.

Key Factors for ESL and Science

Current approaches to science and second language education based on results of both research and classroom practice indicate a set of central notions for relating science and ESL. Evidence presented in this chapter gives particular emphasis to the following reasons why science inquiry can facilitate development of ESL:

1. Science provides the sociocognitive conflict that spurs development of a new language system.

2. Science provides a source of meaningful and relevant language input, using hands-on materials and texts with extralinguistic devices (diagrams, charts, pictures, other visuals) to clarify meaning.

3. Science provides the positive affective conditions of high motivation and low anxiety.

4. Science labs provide extensive opportunities for small-group interactions in which students negotiate meanings and receive comprehensible language input.

5. Science provides opportunities for heterogeneous grouping with the role of peer tutor alternating among students, factors that contribute to input, interaction, and a positive affective climate.

6. Science provides experience with a wide range of language functions.

7. Science leads to extensive vocabulary development needed for school success.

8. Science integrates all modalities of language use: listening, speaking, reading, and writing.

9. Science provides literacy-related tasks for development of cognitive/academic language proficiency.

10. Science uses prior cultural and educational experiences for developing new concepts.

All of these factors taken together reflect the optimal conditions provided through science for ESL development. However, classroom integration of science and language education will necessitate changes in current approaches to teacher preparation. For science education to affect ESL as fully as possible, science teachers need an understanding of basic principles in second language acquisition; ESL teachers need experience with basic processes in science inquiry. Although inquiry experiences are integral to effective science programs, they may require structural adjustments in a number of ways in order to promote language development. Both ESL and science teachers need awareness of how to recognize and make use of conditions that facilitate language acquisition in a content area.

Science gives a rich context for genuine language use. From a language acquisition perspective, science as inquiry can serve as a focal point around which oral language and literacy in ESL can develop. In science, the ESL teacher can find the content and conditions to encourage language acquisition. Specifically, from the ESL perspective, science offers:

- interesting, relevant, and challenging content;
- opportunities for students to negotiate meanings;
- an abundance of appropriate language input;
- conditions for keeping students involved;

- material for development of reading;
- activities for development of writing; and
- experiences with the forms and functions of English.

3
ESL and Social Studies Instruction

Melissa King, Barbara Fagan, Terry Bratt, & Rod Baer
Arlington County, Virginia, Public Schools

The ultimate goal of English as a second language (ESL) programs in the elementary and secondary schools is to prepare limited-English-proficient (LEP) students for success in mainstream classes. To achieve this goal, the scope of instruction should be broad enough to embrace the language and the concepts of content-area subjects. Teaching English is not an end in itself, but only a means to an end; the critical outcome is how well teachers equip students to succeed in school (Saville-Troike, 1984). It has been documented that second language students can develop and strengthen language skills while acquiring knowledge and academic skills that are crucial for success in content-area subjects (Lambert & Tucker, 1972). Using language as a vehicle to focus on subject-matter content is an effective way of providing natural exposure to the language.

This chapter addresses the following areas as they relate to ESL and social studies instruction:

- why social studies is or should be a component of ESL instruction;

- curriculum development and program design;

- staff development and teacher training; and

- effective teaching strategies and model lessons.

Language and Content

The language used for academic instruction is clearly different from the language used for social communication. Cummins' (1980) two aspects of language proficiency are: context-embedded, or face-to-face communication, and context-reduced, or academic communicative proficiency. The former is critical in establishing social relations outside the classroom and includes paralinguistic aids to comprehension such as gestures, intonation, objects, and people. The latter (context-reduced) is essential for achievement in academic subjects in school and relies on cognition, conceptual development, and the more formal language used in textbooks and lectures. Research conducted in Canada (Cummins, 1982) revealed that LEP children can reach native-speaker ability in context-embedded proficiency within 2 years. That is, within 2 years of exposure to the target language (English), most children were able to interact socially and affectively with peers and adults. Success in a social context, however, does not guarantee success in an academic environment. For children to perform at a level comparable to that of their English-speaking peers required 5-7 years. There is a considerable gap between the time second language learners are capable of communication and when they are able to function effectively in content-area classes.

In many ESL programs, LEP students are mainstreamed after reaching the "threshold" level by demonstrating social communicative proficiency. The threshold level is the degree of language proficiency needed for survival in a second language environment. It distinguishes between the language skills necessary for basic oral communication and the academic, literacy-related skills used for instructional purposes

(Chamot, 1983) (see Figure 3.1). For LEP students, academic subjects may pose particular problems because they may not have been adequately prepared to deal with the language and skills necessary for content-area subject matter. Clearly, ESL programs can play an active role in promoting the academic language proficiency of LEP students, thereby increasing the rate of success of mainstreamed second language learners. ESL teachers should try to integrate language and communication skills with academic skills and critical thinking. The second language classroom should be viewed as more than a place for children to develop linguistic competence. It should be recognized as a place where students learn how to manipulate, apply, and expand language in order to increase their knowledge of content-area subject matter. It should be recognized as a place where students develop an increasing awareness of how to use what they know in order to understand relationships and solve problems.

It is also evident that mainstream teachers need to become more "language-sensitive" in conducting classes that include nonnative English speakers. Being aware of ESL methods would help these teachers incorporate activities that enhance language development, both oral and written, into content-area lessons. The need for teacher training in content-based English instruction was substantiated by a survey of secondary teachers who considered their top priority to be strategies for ESL instruction in the content areas (McGroarty, 1985).

Chamot (1983) has designed a second language learning model based on Bloom's taxonomy (Bloom & Krathwohl, 1977) of cognitive domains. In this model (see Fig. 3.1, p. 92), each of the six cognitive levels is matched with corresponding linguistic processes, each successive level building on the concepts and skills of the previous one. Both internal (receptive) language skills and external (productive) language skills are outlined for each level. The first three levels— knowledge, comprehension, and application—comprise the survival language skills developed by second language learners as they approach the threshold level. At these stages, students memorize, recombine elements, and use language for real communication. The next three levels—analysis, synthesis, and evaluation—include the academic language skills that are critical in content-area instruction. At these stages, students give and receive information, give explanations, make comparisons, relate ideas, draw conclusions, express judgments, and make decisions.

Cognitive Domain Taxonomy	Linguistic Process	Internal Language Skills	External Language Skills
1 Knowledge	Recalling	Discrimination of and response to sounds, words, and unanalyzed chunks in listening. Identification of labels, letters, phrases in reading.	Production of single words and formulas; imitation of models. Handwriting, spelling, writing of known elements from dictation.
2 Comprehension	Recombining	Recognition of and response to new combinations of known words and phrases in listening and oral reading. Internal translation to and from L_1.	Emergence of interlanguage/telegraphic speech; code-switching and L_1 transfer. Writing from guidelines and recombination dictation.
		------------Social Interaction------------	
3 Application	Communicating	Understanding meaning of what is listened to in informal situations. Emergence of silent reading for basic comprehension.	Communciation of meaning, feelings, and intention in social and highly contextualized situations. Emergence of expository and creative writing.
4 Analysis	Informing	Acquisition of factual information from listening and reading in decontextualized situations.	Application of factual information acquired to formal, academic speaking and writing activities.
5 Synthesis	Generalizing	Use of information acquired through reading and listening to find relationships; make inferences, draw conclusions.	Explanation of relationships, inferences, and conclusions through formal speech and writing.
6 Evaluation	Judging	Evaluation of accuracy, value, and applicability of ideas acquired through reading and listening.	Expression of judgments through speech and writing, use of rhetorical conventions.

Figure 3.1. Second Language Learning Model

Note. From "Toward a Functional ESL Curriculum in the Elementary School" by A.U. Chamot, 1983, *TESOL Quarterly, 17,* p. 462. Copyright 1983 by Teachers of English to Speakers of Other Languages. Reprinted by permission.

Chamot's Second Language Learning Model is developmental in nature and provides a basic framework for skills progression. The designated threshold level separates social from academic proficiency. Going beyond the threshold level, there is a high degree of correlation between the highest three levels and the critical thinking skills that are emphasized in social studies instruction. Students are often required to draw conclusions, make inferences, determine relationships, and make comparisons in historical contexts. Furthermore, the vocabulary and concepts presented in social studies lessons provide a natural means for developing higher-level thinking skills. The terminology and factual information become the vehicles for building concepts and stimulating divergent thinking in social studies lessons.

Integrating Language and Content

Learning is a holistic process that cannot be compartmentalized. Too often, specific skills are isolated and taught outside of meaningful contexts, making it difficult for the learner to "reassemble" the whole picture in applying the skills for real purposes. Language teaching and learning should be an integrated and systematic process that provides meaningful content (Titone, 1981). Integrated language arts instruction develops oral and written communication simultaneously, fostering the development of all language skills in meaningful contexts. In contrast, ESL lessons that focus only on structural patterns, for example, appear to contribute little to students' eventual success in academic programs (Saville-Troike, 1984).

Furthermore, subject-matter content can and should be interwoven into language lessons. Anderson, Hiebert, Scott, and Wilkenson (1984) state that the most logical place for instruction in reading and thinking strategies is in social studies and science, rather than in separate lessons about reading. Although the integration of reading and subject-matter instruction is not a new idea, there is little indication that such integration is commonly practiced.

Asher (1982) and Carroll (1967) have documented the beneficial effects of natural language exposure for second language acquisition. Social studies content provides opportunities for natural language learning, allowing the learner to focus on the content or meaning rather than on the structure of the language. For example, after students have learned about the voyages and discoveries of various European explorers, they may be asked to express points of comparison among them both orally and in written form. Using flashcards that give key information about each explorer, the teacher can help students form specific sentence constructions to express comparison. Following are some sample sentence patterns:

> Columbus was a Spanish explorer, and so was Balboa.
> Columbus was a Spanish explorer, and Balboa was too.
> Both Columbus and Balboa were Spanish explorers.

Students see an immediate application of the linguistic structures and will be able to make similar comparisons in future lessons.

New information presented in social studies lessons is often a catalyst for further academic and language learning. The motivation for language learning arises naturally as students become involved in understanding concepts of history, geography, culture, and so on. At the same time, social studies knowledge strengthens and enriches an increased awareness of self, the community, and the environment. A lesson on westward movement in the United States in the 1980s, for example, may activate students' interest in migration patterns throughout U.S. history. This knowledge may also lead them to discover more about recent immigants and where they have settled, and eventually to explore how they themselves fit into these patterns of movement as newcomers to the United States.

The Role of Background Knowledge

Social studies plays an important role in the acculturation process of LEP students. When they first come to the United States, they are expected to participate in classroom settings and to operate within a society that they do not fully understand. Because they may not be aware of American rules and behavioral expectations, language-minority students are at a disadvantage. LEP students bring with them their cultural framework for social interaction, as well as subconscious assumptions about acceptable behavior and belief systems. Culture is the context within which people think, exist, feel, and relate to others (Brown, 1980), representing a blueprint for personal and social existence. People unconsciously learn what to notice, what not to notice, how to divide time and space, how to relate to other people, how to handle responsibility, and, to some extent, whether experience is seen as whole or fragmented. Because their values may be dramatically different from North American values, foreign students may encounter confusion and conflict trying to adjust to life in the United States. A social studies class can give LEP students an introduction to the American experience, helping them to understand American values and relationships with the outside world.

LEP students, naturally, are as unaware of their assumptions as anyone; each culture has its own reality (Hall, 1976). These students can never participate fully in American society unless they understand the American reality. It is not an exaggeration to say that one of the ESL teacher's greatest responsibilities is to give students tools that enable them to function effectively in society.

An ESL/social studies class should be concerned with more than historical facts, geography, and terminology. It can promote the development of critical concepts of American history, thereby helping culturally different students to understand their new country and its origins. In an ESL/social studies class, students can learn about the spirit of independence and the sense of individualism that characterizes American behavior. They can study U.S. laws and institutions that are, in fact, a reflection of American people. They can identify with the colonists' struggles for freedom and appreciate the significance of the Bill of Rights as a protection of this freedom. Students can discover how the U.S. government functions and what is expected of responsible citizens. Indeed, the ESL/social studies class can be a support system for LEP students who are trying to adjust to a new culture. In expanding their knowledge, the students envision a more realistic picture of the new culture and how they might operate within it. A more positive attitude and concept of self in turn enhances language proficiency (Oller, Baca, & Vigil, 1978).

Curriculum Development and Program Design

At the elementary and secondary levels, the ESL curriculum must reflect the mainstream curriculum. If students are to be prepared to cope with the academic mainstream, they must acquire not only the language skills, but also the critical thinking and study skills required in content-area classes. The locally designed curricula of most school districts correlate with adopted texts. Generally, schools set grade-level objectives by subject area that students must master as they progress through the system. School districts with large LEP populations have experienced difficulties in efforts to tailor content-area instruction to meet the needs of second-language students. The following problems have become evident:

• LEP students may not have had social studies instruction in their native countries.

• Social studies concepts may not have been adequately developed in classes LEP students have attended previously.

• The content of American social studies instruction may differ greatly from that of other countries (there may be gaps in students' knowledge).

• LEP students may lack the English-language skills needed to participate on grade level in social studies classes.

• Social studies materials are often too difficult for beginning and intermediate LEP students (texts assume a specific reading level for each grade).

• Teachers may feel unprepared to integrate ESL and social studies instruction (mainstream teachers need training in ESL methodology, and ESL teachers need content-area preparation).

• LEP students are unfamiliar with social studies vocabulary and have trouble keeping pace with native-English-speaking students who have a broad vocabulary base in social studies.

• The cumulative nature of social studies often creates situations in which LEP students fail to grasp concepts or ideas because they have missed previous instruction.

Integrating ESL and social studies instruction is by no means easy, but the advantages are clear. LEP students who progress in both language and content-area skills simultaneously will make a smoother transition into the mainstream. Programs that make a firm commitment to integrated ESL and social studies instruction may find that LEP students demonstrate greater gains overall and require less actual time in special English-language classes. Results from additional research are needed to verify this generalization.

Curriculum Development

Curriculum development is a major concern of proponents of ESL/social studies instruction. Administrators and teachers need to find ways to create meaningful learning situations that build on previously acquired knowledge and are realistic for the culturally different and LEP student. Through meaningful learning, new material becomes an integral part of existing cognitive structures (Ausebel, 1963). F. Smith (1975) contends that a learning situation can be meaningful only if the learner can relate the new learning task to prior knowledge and if the task itself is related to an existing knowledge structure. For the teacher of social studies, this idea is extremely important. For the teacher of social studies classes with LEP students who come from a wide variety of backgrounds, developing this idea becomes an awesome challenge. Is there a viable solution? One of the most effective approaches seems to be one that makes few assumptions about students' prior knowledge of social studies. Teachers should start with the most basic concepts and gradually develop related ideas into broader units of study.

Rather than adapting a fifth-grade textbook for fifth-grade LEP students, the teacher may want to develop a series of lessons that incorporate important concepts from grades one through four or five. Students who have not yet grasped concepts introduced at an earlier level may experience difficulty with the fifth-grade social studies curriculum. To ensure more depth of understanding, particularly as it relates to historical developments and social studies concepts, teachers may need to adopt an approach that is comprehensive and cumulative in nature. This does not imply a "watered-down" approach, but stresses the need for the learner to be given an opportunity to acquire new knowledge in a meaningful and relevant fashion, rather than in a piecemeal approach.

Many of the significant events and historical developments covered in social studies lessons can be related to fundamental concepts that may apply to a variety of situations and settings. Before beginning a unit on the American Civil War, for example, the teacher should discuss the idea that differences can eventually lead to conflict. Students may well understand this concept from their own personal experiences. This understanding can be extended into an exploration of their awareness of social, political, and economic differences among groups of people and nationalities. The teacher can then focus on specific facts related to differences between the North and South in the antebellum period, which eventually led to the Civil War. A basic concept can thus become the starting point for a social studies unit. An appreciation of such fundamental concepts and their role throughout history is an essential component of social studies instruction. Students who memorize facts and figures, but fail to comprehend the important concepts, will not really master the content of social studies. In addition, by relating the current unit of study to the students' own background knowledge, the teacher promotes understanding and stimulates enthusiasm for the topic. ESL students, for example, may not be keenly interested in the Confederacy in the 1860s, but they will probably be anxious to discuss their own personal problems with being "different." The teacher capitalizes on these experiences by tying them into the social studies concept and the events leading up to the Civil War.

It is important to understand that the content-based ESL curricula are *not* a substitute for the mainstream curricula, but are a preparation for them. The language of the modified curricula may be simplified, but not at the exclusion of higher-level thinking skills. Curriculum developers should examine the requirements of the mainstream curricula and determine which objectives are essential for academic success. ESL and social studies teachers can plan staff development activities that enable them to share strategies and resources in order to implement the curricula in the most effective and efficient way possible. Quite often, curriculum writers of ESL/social studies programs develop model lesson plans to illustrate how teachers can relate content-area information while reinforcing language and communication skills. No matter how much advance planning is done, however, it is during the actual implementation process that a great deal is discovered about integrating ESL and social studies instruction. Teachers' real experiences help them to understand and assimilate successful instructional practices.

Other school systems with large concentrations of language-minority students have elected not to separate these learners from native speakers in the content-area classes. Instead, mainstream teachers have been trained in ESL methods and provided with adapted curricular materials for the second language students. In Fairfax County, Virginia, the close collaboration between ESL teachers and social studies teachers has created an effective instructional setting for LEP students. In such situations, however, it is imperative that educators from the two disciplines work closely together to provide a balanced, methodologically sound social studies program for these special-needs students.

Choosing a Program

Generally speaking, the specific type of ESL/social studies program that is adopted by any school district depends on several variables: the size of the LEP population, the distribution of the LEP students throughout the district, the educational backgrounds of these students, the human resources available, the specific expertise of staff members, mandated requirements of the school system, and the amount of financial support available. Because no two school districts' needs and resources are identical, a variety of solutions to the problems of ESL learners in social studies classes has arisen. Indeed, it is extremely important that any system assess its own needs before implementing a new program, whether it is an entirely novel idea or one that is patterned after other model programs already in operation.

School systems with large and growing numbers of language-minority students may opt for some type of content-based ESL instruction that places the ESL learners in special or "sheltered" social studies courses. Locally designed curricula may provide the instructional framework for such classes. The curricula are based on the mainstream curriculum with grade-level objectives and specific exit criteria. Textbooks with a lower reading level are used so that the LEP student can comprehend reading material but still benefit from the necessary application of study skills in such content-area texts. When the proficiency level of the second language learners precludes the use of such texts, adapted materials are used. Development of simplified instructional materials requires considerable time and creative talent, but without adequate teaching materials, the success of the ESL/social studies classes may be undermined. Experienced teachers have also discovered that lower grade-level supplements to social studies programs are often appropriate.

School systems with smaller LEP student populations may choose to keep these learners in the mainstream, providing them with additional support as needed. Specially trained social studies teachers can be highly effective, and the influence of the native English speakers on language acquisition cannot be understated. In these situations, community volunteers (perhaps bilingual) and peer tutors may be a possibility well worth exploring. These paraprofessionals and student teachers can provide valuable individualized assistance to the language-minority students.

Model Programs

School districts with a heavy influx of second language learners have begun to look toward content-based ESL instruction as a viable and preferable approach for educating LEP students. Several different program designs have been developed and implemented. In the Arlington (VA) Public Schools, a tremendous influx of language-minority students in the 1970s led to unique problems. Not only did these students require extra help in learning to speak, read, and write in English, but they also needed additional support in order to function in content-area classes. The fact that many of these newcomers were deficient in previous schooling experience compounded the difficulties they encountered in American classrooms.

The High Intensity Language Training (HILT) program was developed in Arlington to serve the language-minority students in grades one through 12. At both the elementary and secondary levels, the HILT program provides instruction in mathematics, science, and social studies as well as language and communication. The purpose of the content-area classes is to expand students' knowledge of vocabulary and concepts while strengthening the study skills and critical thinking skills necessary for success in content classes in the mainstream. By preparing students with the academic "prerequisites" and by exposing them to key concepts and terminology, the HILT program helps second language learners feel more comfortable in mainstream classes and boosts their chances to excel in subjects such as U.S. history and government.

The HILT program in El Paso, Texas, follows a similar approach in preparing LEP students for the mainstream. In this program, students are first enrolled in special English classes that teach content-area vocabulary and concepts. The second phase is "sheltered" content-area courses, which are grade-appropriate but designed for second language learners. Finally, the students are placed into mainstream classes with their English-speaking peers.

In the state of California, "sheltered" English and content-area courses are being implemented in many school districts. Sheltered English is a teaching method in which core curriculum (mathematics, reading, social studies, etc.) is presented to LEP students using special techniques to ensure that the content is understood. Instructors may modify lessons (breaking down content information), simplify language, make use of a variety of visual aids, encourage student involvement, and make frequent checks for comprehension. Beginning LEP students receive ESL instruction as well as sheltered mathematics and science. The San Diego City Schools English for LEP Students (ELEPS) program includes a comprehensive outline of topics that develop basic skills as well as the content areas. Instructional materials for sheltered social studies classes have been locally designed, and sample units are available upon request. Educators have expressed widespread satisfaction with the sheltered-English program in terms of gains in student knowledge of subject matter and overall progress in second language acquisition.

Program Evaluation

Evaluation of the effectiveness of ESL programs and of LEP students' progress is critical to continued improvement and success, but the method and instruments used for evaluation require careful scrutiny. By virtue of the fact that their English is limited, LEP students do not perform as well as mainstream students on standardized tests such as the SRA (Science Research Associates) and the California Achievement Tests. Furthermore, differences and deficiencies in educational backgrounds and experiences contribute to the difficulties LEP students have with standardized tests. On the other hand, standardized test results can provide helpful evaluative and comparative information regarding LEP students' progress.

Content-based ESL programs must provide for some assessment of student mastery of specific program and curricular objectives. This assessment must recur and be consistent from year to year. Such evaluative information and feedback is absolutely necessary for appropriate curricular and programmatic decisions. Evaluation is the foundation for future planning, ongoing improvement, and modifications.

Unfortunately, few testing instruments are available that might be used to evaluate LEP students' social studies knowledge. Most school districts use locally developed tests to monitor students' progress, but few, if any, attempts have been made to collect substantive data for statistical purposes. It is hoped that further research and collaboration among educators will result in some standardized evaluation instruments for this purpose.

Staff Development and Teacher Training

Regardless of decisions made for curriculum development and program implementation, the key to successful learning on the student's part is the teacher. It is absolutely essential that teachers of ESL/social studies classes have knowledge of second language acquisition and ESL methodology. These teachers also need to become familiar with the cultural backgrounds of their students and to develop sensitivity in working with culturally different learners in the school setting. These teachers will need to increase their awareness of various learning styles and their influence on language acquisition. Teachers of ESL/social studies classes need opportunities to share ideas and experiences with other teachers, as well as sufficient time to explore new instructional strategies, materials, and resources. Staff development is a necessary component for any school with an LEP population, particularly if curricular or program innovations are being instituted to serve this LEP population.

One way to meet these curricula and staff needs is through the formation of "technical teams." The purpose of a technical team is to develop curricula and materials for an ESL program and provide staff development in response to program needs identified by teachers. Each need is defined, the tasks necessary to meet the need are outlined, and the needed product is produced on an ongoing basis by the technical team. While the curricula and materials are being developed, staff development is provided through team interaction, demonstration, and training provided by staff members and consultants. Much of the planning for curriculum revision is done during the school year, while the actual writing of curriculum guides and teaching materials is completed during the summer months.

In Arlington, for example, a group of teachers working with beginning speakers of English at the secondary level identified a need for social studies materials written on a primer/first grade level. This group met for a brainstorming session on what needed to be developed and how. By the end of this session, a technical team had been formed and was ready to begin work. It was decided that a social studies reader with an accompanying consumable workbook would be developed. The team also decided that it would survey K-4 social studies texts written for native speakers in order to decide what concepts and vocabulary needed to be included. When this task was completed, the team began to write units. A teacher with artistic talents was invited to join the team so that the materials would be illustrated. The materials were completed during a summer curriculum project and piloted during the following school year. The team surveyed the teachers who had used the pilot materials and made appropriate revisions on the basis of the teachers' comments. Little was changed in the way of content or illustration, but it was decided to make the workbook a two-part series. A detailed teacher's guide was also developed. Five years later, these social studies materials are still in use, and teacher satisfaction with them is high.

Effective Teaching Strategies

The experiences of Arlington's ESL/social studies teachers since the inception of the HILT program have contributed to an increased awareness of 'what works' in these content-area classes. Specific teaching strategies have proven to be highly effective in reaching LEP students. Some of these strategies are discussed in the following section, with practical suggestions for incorporating these strategies into social studies lessons included in the discussion. These strategies were not devised strictly as ESL methods. They are intended to show how teachers can adapt some conventional instructional activities to take "language advantage" of social studies lessons. The strategies illustrate how teachers can readily use social studies content to enhance language development, and, conversely, how teachers can use language classes as a means of expanding social studies knowledge. It is evident that content-area subject matter provides a rich body of knowledge through which creative instructional activities may emerge.

Use of Manipulatives and Multimedia Materials

ESL programs that include a social studies component must create a learning environment rich in multimedia materials and manipulatives. Many of the concepts presented in social studies lessons are abstract ideas that may be particularly difficult for nonnative students. Pictures provide students with visual experiences that transcend language barriers. For example, describing a scene from an old western mining town in the 1850s is simply not the same as showing a photograph or picture of the scene. When language proficiency is a problem, verbal or written descriptions are inadequate and need to be supplemented with pictorial representations. The visual image makes an immediate impression on the viewer and does not rely solely on an oral or written explanation that may elude LEP students. Without such visual experiences, teachers cannot know whether they have reached all students with important ideas and information.

Real objects or historical artifacts that reinforce social studies concepts provide students with tactile as well as visual experiences. Concrete objects bring ideas to life and make learning exciting and fun. By including kinesthetic activities in content-area lessons, the teacher may reach students who are at the lowest level of English proficiency and those who are predominantly experiential learners. A discussion of the common tools and household objects of the early 18th century, for example, does not have the same impact as a display and demonstration of these objects and how they were used. Such a display and demonstration is a memorable experience that students can relate to new vocabulary and concepts.

A wide variety of media materials for social studies is available in most public school libraries. Large-sized study prints and picture sets keyed to specific themes are useful for relating information and stimulating thinking in the classroom. Filmstrips are easily adapted for use with LEP students because the teacher can take advantage of the visual experience while altering the actual text to accommodate for different levels of English proficiency. Numerous 16mm films for social studies are also available but must be chosen with care because the language is often beyond what LEP students can comprehend. Ideas presented in films depicting historical events or processes may make reading and writing assignments associated with these ideas less difficult to process (Sinatra & Stahl-Gemake, 1983). In addition, periodicals such as "National Geographic" serve as excellent supplementary resources for social studies lessons. Vivid photographs and current themes make such resources a perfect complement to other instructional materials.

Language Experiences

Shared experiences initiate the desire for communication. In the ESL classroom, the teacher can use concrete experiences as stimuli for language development. In the traditional language experience approach, the teacher encourages spontaneous language from students that eventually becomes the foundation for a written story (Lee & Allen, 1963). Because LEP students may have extremely limited abilities in spontaneous oral English, the teacher may want to adapt this approach. In an adapted language experience lesson, the teacher becomes a participant in an activity with the students. In advance, she targets specific vocabulary, structures, and concepts to incorporate into the lesson, and during the active experience she elicits this language from students. Throughout the experience both spontaneous and guided language are evident, and literacy skills are encouraged with the use of flashcards and sentence strips for language produced. A story created by the class with the teacher's help is a natural follow-up.

Social studies lessons lend themselves well to this approach. In a unit on democratic government, for example, the teacher may want to stage an election of class officers to illustrate voting procedures and the concept of representative democracy. During and after the election, the class can discuss the process and the teacher can help them put their ideas into writing. The experience itself makes an impact on the students, helps clarify meaning, and assists in long-term memory. Research on the kinesthetic memory system indicates that when the body is actively involved in the learning process, ideas and concepts are integrated rapidly. Learning by doing is highly effective (Wayman, 1985).

The following hypothetical example is included to illustrate how an ESL/social studies teacher can turn to experiences to clarify the meaning of new concepts.

In an intermediate-level ESL social studies class studying the role of the Constitutional Convention in writing the U.S. Constitution, the concept of reaching compromises to make decisions may be an entirely new idea. The social studies teacher needs to determine whether the students can either recall aspects from their own experiences that might be similar, such as the various lawmaking bodies of their countries. If the students do not clearly understand this topic, then the teacher must create an experience that the students can draw from later. For example, the students could role-play various scenes from colonial times, when power was concentrated in the hands of a few. They could represent different interest groups, each arguing to have certain laws passed. With the teacher as facilitator, the students will come to understand that they must compromise or give up certain wants if any progress is to be achieved. Once the students have understood the concept of compromise, the teacher can proceed with the lesson on the Constitution and how its laws were created.

Managing Multilevel Classes

Most ESL and classroom teachers have experienced the difficulty of working with multilevel classes. The range of abilities can be as great as four or five reading grade levels. Teachers feel that many subjects must be taught in small groups in order to meet individual needs. However, the wide range of English proficiency levels does not completely preclude total-group instruction. Because many social studies lessons may be in the form of directed teaching and discussion, they provide excellent opportunities for involving the whole class. Students at lower proficiency levels benefit from the exposure to the language provided by the more advanced students during oral language activities and discussions. Students at advanced levels benefit from the increased amount of reinforcement of vocabulary and concepts that is provided for beginning-level students.

Creative drama, role-playing, hands-on experiences, field trips and music and art projects are some of the many activities that can be implemented in the multilevel ESL/social studies classroom. These activities challenge and enrich all students, regardless of language proficiency in English. Because of differing language and ability levels, students may not come away from a lesson or activity with exactly the same gains in knowledge, but they all will have benefited from the experiences.

Directed Reading Thinking Activity

The Directed Reading Thinking Activity (DRTA) is a highly effective strategy that can be applied in social studies lessons for LEP students. The three main steps of a DRTA are to predict, to read, and to prove. These steps motivate students to apply higher-level thinking skills. By brainstorming with the class before reading about a specific topic, the teacher finds out how much the students already know about that topic. This strategy is especially useful with ESL classes because of the variety and range to be found in their background knowledge and experiences. By encouraging students to predict what might be in the reading, the teacher asks students to call on prior knowledge that might be useful in this assignment. Students are immediately involved in the topic through oral discussion and are anxious to make appropriate "guesses" about what will be in the reading. As they read, students may have to revise their predictions, and they are challenged to make corrections in their own assumptions, weighing and evaluating what they know with what they read. In so doing, old information is assimilated into new information, and cognitive growth occurs. The teacher guides students through this activity and follows up on the reading with questions to check comprehension of subject matter. By this means, the teacher can find out how much the students actually understood and how well they can respond to probes of the subject matter.

The DRTA might be used for a lesson on immigration to the United States in the early 20th century. Before assigning a reading, the teacher may discuss ESL students' own experiences with immigration. The class might then discuss all the photographs or pictures presented with the reading. They should compare and contrast their personal experiences with what is depicted. Then they might read through the passage in a step-by-step manner with the teacher, stopping at appropriate places to make predictions about what might follow. Finally, the teacher will help the students to discover how accurate their predictions were and to summarize what they have read.

Semantic Webbing

Outlining and note-taking are advanced study skills that require students to summarize important ideas in specific formats. LEP students often have trouble developing outlines and taking notes because they must comprehend the entire message (given orally or in writing) before they can extract the main ideas and important details and arrange them in an appropriate form. Semantic webbing is an extremely helpful way to teach students how to perceive relationships and integrate information and concepts within the context of a main idea or topic (Freedman & Reynolds, 1980). The graphic representation afforded students by semantic webbing bridges the gap between concrete images and more abstract ideas. The core of a web is a key question or term that establishes the purpose of the reading or topic for discussion. Following an oral discussion or a reading, students construct web strands and web supports by putting key words or phrases in boxes or in some other visual arrangement. The boxes can then be connected to illustrate relationships or subheadings under the main idea(s). Such a visual scheme highlights important ideas and categories, greatly aiding overall comprehension.

An example of semantic webbing follows:

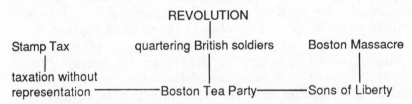

In this diagram, students list events and key words about the Revolution in a web format. This web can be extended to include new information and additional details. Students can order events chronologically to show sequence, or draw diagrams to show cause-and-effect relationships. The web serves as a graphic model that stimulates students to expand on their own ideas in formulating concepts. For learners who have difficulty perceiving relationships between main ideas and details, the spatial arrangement helps crystallize the concepts.

SQ4R

The SQ4R method (Robinson, 1962) is an effective means for teaching students how to outline new information presented in a specific chapter in a social studies text. It is highly recommended that students develop skills in using this method early in the year, because it encourages them to organize and summarize new information systematically and independently. Its value for LEP students is that it teaches them a specific and routine method for breaking down difficult reading material. The steps for SQ4R are the survey, questions, and reading, reciting, recording, and reviewing.

Survey. Students skim the chapter for an overview of topics and material. They read subtopics, look at visuals and graphs, and read highlighted vocabulary.

Questions. Students fold notebook paper in half (vertically). On the left side, they list any questions that come to mind about the first subheading in the chapter, thereby establishing a purpose for reading. For example:

Spain's Empire Grows [subheading]

- *Where was Spain's empire?*
- *What lands were in the empire?*
- *How did the empire grow?*
- *When did this happen?*

Reading. Students read the text under this subheading to learn about the new topic and to answer the questions they had.

Reciting. Students try to answer as many of their own questions as possible from information gained from the reading. These responses should be oral in order to reinforce the new information.

Recording. Students write down answers to their questions, making the transfer from oral to written language.

Reviewing. Students immediately review what they have written. Then they are ready to move on to the next subheading and repeat the SQ4R process.

By continuing through the chapter with this method, the students will have created their own study sheet containing pertinent information about the chapter. The folded question sheets they have developed can be used by the teacher to test students on new material, providing a means of evaluative feedback.

SQ4R motivates students to deal with new information independently and efficiently while strengthening their note-taking skills. For LEP students in mainstream classes, this is one approach to difficult social studies texts that present heavy loads of new concepts and vocabulary.

Paraphrasing and Summarizing

Limited English proficiency will undoubtedly hamper students when they take notes in class, answer essay questions, and write reports. Moreover, reproducing lessons learned by rote or material produced by copying (methods many students used in their native schools) is unacceptable in most American classrooms. Therefore, paraphrasing and summarizing are essential skills for LEP students. Too often, teachers assume students will develop these skills independently, when, in fact, these skills must be taught and reinforced through repeated practice.

One activity that shows students how ideas can be restated is called "Who said this?" After teaching a unit on the causes of the American Revolution, the teacher gives students a list of statements and asks them to identify the speaker of each one as either King George or Thomas Jefferson. Sample sentences could be, *I refuse to pay taxes if I can't elect my own leader* or *I insist that the colonists pay a higher tax on tea.* After students have labeled the statements by speaker, they can list the reasons for their answers. Students should be told that they are actually paraphrasing what they have read. As a follow-up activity, students can write three sentences that summarize the causes of the American Revolution. LEP students at a more advanced level could be asked to write a chapter summary by first skimming each paragraph for the main idea and jotting it down. They might then restate the idea in their own words and use these restatements for a chapter summary.

Writing in the Content Areas

Social studies lends itself well to the development of writing skills. Recognizing that there are different levels of response in writing, teachers can incorporate various expository writing activities into social studies lessons. By following the writing process of brainstorming for ideas, organizing, prewriting, proofreading, and rewriting, teachers help students learn how to express themselves on paper. The richness of social studies vocabulary and concepts provides a great deal of content for generative writing. In applying this vocabulary in writing exercises, students also receive reinforcement of grammar and reading skills. Controversial topics that may arise in social studies discussions often stimulate the expression of ideas and personal opinions and can challenge students to write more effectively and persuasively.

Study Skills

Social studies classes afford excellent opportunities for developing students' study skills. Following directions, reading maps and charts, outlining, note-taking, using textbooks, preparing oral and written reports, interpreting cartoons, and using library references are among the skills that can be reinforced in content area lessons. While learning new subject matter, students can apply specific study skills for specific purposes. In so doing, they are not only learning new material, but they are also strengthening skills that are essential for academic success. Social studies content provides a meaningful context for the application of such study skills.

Model Lessons

This section outlines model lessons for elementary and secondary levels. These model lessons are meant to illustrate how a variety of teaching strategies can be combined to create unique experiences that stimulate students' interest and promote the learning process. Teachers are encouraged to experiment with ideas and approaches as they develop their own lessons around social studies themes, for there is no one single best way to teach content-area subjects to language-minority students. The most successful lessons are the ones that incorporate a variety of strategies and activities into carefully planned learning experiences.

Model Lesson—Elementary

Objective

To provide students with an understanding of the origin and traditions of the American Thanksgiving holiday, and to help students develop an appreciation for this holiday as part of American culture.

Grade level

Primary (could also be adapted for upper elementary classes)

Materials

Simple illustrated book on the First Thanksgiving
Pictures of Indians, Pilgrims, Thanksgiving foods, the feast
Construction paper, crayons, scissors, paper bags
Patterns for puppets of Indians and Pilgrims
Samples of Thanksgiving foods

Target vocabulary

Pilgrims	turkey	thankful
Indians	feast	together
Thanksgiving	harvest	celebration

Vocabulary need not be limited to these words during discussions of this lesson, but the teacher will want to make sure that the target vocabulary is clearly illustrated or explained, because these words are crucial to the overall understanding of the lessons.

Procedure

Motivation: The teacher begins with a discussion of celebrations, eliciting responses from students about celebrations they have experienced in their native countries or in the United States. The teacher asks students about the meaning of these celebrations and how they might have changed over time. Teacher asks students what they know about an American Thanksgiving. Words and ideas are written on the board.

Throughout this discussion, the teacher will want to display appropriate pictures and write important vocabulary on the board. The teacher will encourage all students to participate, sharing their enthusiasm for familiar holidays and celebrations. Oral language and aural comprehension are promoted through a lively discussion.

Information: The teacher reads a simple story about the First Thanksgiving, drawing attention to illustrations that help clarify meanings and the concepts being taught. Students are invited to discuss the story and ask questions about words or concepts they do not fully understand. The teacher may conduct some oral drills to reinforce vocabulary or syntax. The teacher will want to find out if this story relates to any of the students' own first-hand experiences. For example, have they ever attended a dinner that honored some other group of people? Have they ever had a dinner to express thanks or appreciation for something or someone?

The teacher may want to show a filmstrip depicting the First Thanksgiving. These pictures will further students' awareness of what conditions were like during this time and motivate them to ask questions. Students can be asked to write down ideas and new words as they view the filmstrip. At the end, they may summarize what they have seen, both orally and in writing.

Practice: The teacher provides materials for students to make paper-bag puppets of Indians and Pilgrims. Students are encouraged to talk as they work on their puppets. When puppets are completed, students role-play parts as Indians and Pilgrims, reenacting the First Thanksgiving. The teacher may want to provide sample dialogues if students have trouble getting started on this activity. Students can be paired up to give them maximum opportunities for dialogue.

The teacher then shows students some samples of typical

Thanksgiving foods such as cranberry sauce, corn bread, pumpkin pie, and so on. The teacher talks about how these foods are made and where they come from. Students explore the foods by smelling, tasting, and touching (for sense of texture) them. The teacher elicits descriptive adjectives in the discussion of these foods, and students tell whether or not they like the foods. All such activity generates language and stimulates vocabulary development.

Enrichment and extension: The teacher may want to set up a language experience activity in which students make some of the Thanksgiving foods (pumpkin pie, for example). Throughout the activity, the teacher prompts students to practice vocabulary and sentence patterns, using flashcards and sentence strips as needed visual reinforcement. Students learn a specific sequence of steps for making the food(s) and are then able to give simple directions for the procedure(s).

The teacher may want to try having an in-class Thanksgiving dinner. Students participate in preparing foods and setting the table. Students also share ideas about being thankful, perhaps writing down some of their ideas to exchange with classmates. Following the minicelebration, students can write simple descriptions of the preparation and actual dinner.

Integration with Other Subject Areas

Mathematics—Students learn the song "Ten Little Indians" and do simple word problems with Thanksgiving vocabulary.

Science—Teacher reviews the four food groups, and students learn which Thanksgiving foods fit into each category.

Reading/writing—Students make "pictionaries" of Thanksgiving words, using alphabetization and spelling skills.

Art and drama—Students make simple costumes and stage a simple production of the First Thanksgiving.

Model Lesson—Secondary

Objective

To provide students with an understanding of why Spain decided to explore the New World, and to learn about the explorations of Columbus, Magellan, Balboa, and other Spanish explorers.

Grade level

Secondary ESL/social studies class

Materials

Large wall map, flashcards, yarn

Target vocabulary

voyage	colony	navigation
empire	explore	claim

Procedure

Motivation: Using a large wall map, the teacher and students review trade routes used by Italian states and other European countries in the 1400s for trading with India and China. Students brainstorm as to why Spain would want to find an alternate route. Teacher should accept all responses, such as: *Spain wants to get rich. Spain wants to be famous. Spain wants to be powerful.* (In this case, the teacher may want to ask the students to turn the statements into the past tense.) Students will practice and develop linguistic skills by agreeing or disagreeing with the reasons given. This activity may be done in small groups to maximize individual students' oral participation.

This part of the lesson is essential because it stimulates students to become involved in the new ideas. It also allows the teacher to find out how much background information the students have related to this topic.

Information: The teacher uses the students' predictions and ideas from the motivation section as a basis for presenting new information about Spanish exploration. The teacher may want to present each new explorer with flashcards that give explorer's name, dates of discoveries, and the area explored. Students will need to refer to a wall map to trace the paths of exploration and may find it helpful to use different colored yarn pieces to show where explorers traveled. Students can tell *who* explored, *where* they went, *when* they went, and *why* they explored.

After the new material is presented orally and visually, the teacher has students skim the headings and subheadings of a reading, such as a chapter in a textbook that covers this unit. This is the "survey" part of the SQ4R Method. This technique may be used so that students can create a study sheet related to the new information. After the students have completed this sheet, the teacher should review each subheading in the reading to check for basic comprehension. Students may be asked to state the main idea of the reading and to locate specific sentences that support their answers. New vocabulary pertaining to the exploration unit is emphasized throughout the lesson, and students are encouraged to use context clues whenever possible to understand anything unfamiliar.

The teacher may want to show a filmstrip or movie about the Spanish explorers to reinforce new concepts.

Practice

The students now need to review new vocabulary and concepts that they have learned in the chapter. This is an appropriate time for some type of evaluation: Both short answers and essay questions would show an understanding of the new material. For example, students can write a paragraph describing Columbus' voyages, construct a chart listing dates, explorers, and routes the explorers used, or describe why Spain decided to explore westward.

Enrichment and extension: Students need to have a chance to choose an activity that will enable them to enrich their understanding of Spanish explorers. They are building on new information they have recently learned, and they now need to apply it to a new situation. Some possible activities to foster this extension of their learning are:

• Students conduct research in the library on a Spanish explorer to find out the route traveled, problems encountered, discoveries, and so on. This information can be filled in on a chart or completed on a poster.

• Students role-play Spanish explorers in a panel discussion. The teacher acts as moderator and poses leading questions such as *Tell us, Mr. Columbus, what problems did you encounter on your voyages?* All students will benefit from participating and listening to the responses.

• Students can pretend they are explorers who want to find new land. They must describe where they want to sail, how they would raise funds, what they hope to find, and so on. This can be a writing activity or an oral discussion.

Conclusion

In summary, it is clear that using social studies content as a medium for second language instruction may greatly enhance and accelerate LEP students' language acquisition, as well as assist in the acculturation process. School districts with established and/or growing numbers of LEP students are encouraged to consider instituting classes that integrate the teaching of language and communication skills with subject matter content.

Instructional Resources

Recommended instructional materials for ESL/social studies classes follow.

Publisher	Type of Resource
Linmore Publishing Company P.O. Box 1545 Palatine, IL 60078	Textbook for LEP students— *Content Area ESL: Social Studies* by Dennis Terdy
Roger Olsen and Lynn Reer 1282 29th Ave. San Francisco, CA 94122	Prepublication manuscript of a series of beginning-level social studies lessons that promote language development— *History Helpers*
Creative Associates ESL/Bilingual Education Project 1901 N. Moore St., Suite 920 Arlington, VA 22209	Staff development materials and technical assistance
Steck Vaugh Company P.O. Box 2028 Austin, TX 78768	Social studies materials written at a lower reading level with language arts activities to supplement them
Modern Curriculum Press 13900 Prospect Rd. Cleveland, OH 44136	
Milliken c/o Kurz, Inc. 207 E. Patapsco Ave. Baltimore, MD 21225	
Frank Schaffer 26616 Indian Peak Rd.	Spirit masters and supplementary study skills workbooks

Dept. 46
Rancho Palos Verde, CA 92074

Curriculum Associates
5 Esquire Rd.
North Billerica, MA 01862

Hayes School Publishing Company
P.O. Box 187
Belmont, NC 28012

O'Malley & Chamot
Fairfax County ESL
  Content-Area Program

Curriculum guide—"U.S. and
Virginia Government for ESL
Students"

Addison-Wesley

*Language Development Through
Content*

M. Maggs

English Across the Curriculum
(very good for beginners)

Arlington County Public Schools
ESOL Program
1426 N. Quincy St.
Arlington, VA 22207

Curriculum guides and adapted
social studies materials

San Diego City Schools
Second Language Office
4100 Normal St.
San Diego, CA 92103

Sample units from sheltered-
English courses

References

Aiken, L.R. (1971). Verbal factors and math learning: A review of research. *Journal for Research in Mathematics Education, 2*, 304-313.

Alatis, J.E., Altman, H.B., & Alatis, P.M. (1981). *The second language classroom: Directions for the 1980s.* New York: Oxford University Press.

Anderson, R., Hiebert, E., Scott, J., & Wilkenson, S. (1984). *Becoming a nation of readers: The report of the Commission of Reading.* Washington, DC: U.S. Dept. of Education.

Asher, J.J. (1982). *Learning another language through actions* (2nd ed.). Los Gatos, CA: Sky Oaks Productions.

Ausebel, D.A. (1963). Cognitive structure and the facilitation of meaningful verbal learning. *Journal of Teacher Education, 14,* 217-221.

Beebe, L.M. (1983). Risk-taking and the language learner. In H.W. Seliger & M.H. Long (Eds.), *Classroom oriented research in second language acquisition* (pp. 39-66). Rowley, MA: Newbury House.

Bickel, C., Eigenfeld, N., & Hogg, J. (1973). *Physical science investigations.* Boston, MA: Houghton Mifflin.

Bloom, B., & Krathwohl, D. (1977). *Taxonomy of educational objectives: Handbook I: Cognitive Domain.* New York: Longman.

Brown, H.D. (1980). *Principles of language learning and teaching.* Englewood Cliffs, NJ: Prentice-Hall.

Bullock Committee (1975). *A language for life.* London: Dept. of Education and Sciences, HMSO.

Burton, L. (1984). Mathematical thinking: The struggle for meaning. *Journal for Research in Mathematics Education, 15,* 35-49.

Bye, M.P. (1975). *Reading in math and cognitive development.* Unpublished manuscript. (ERIC Document Reproduction Service No. ED 124 926).

Calkins, M. (1986). *The art of teaching writing.* Portsmouth, NH: Heinemann Educational Books.

Carroll, J.B. (1967). Foreign language proficiency levels attained by language majors near graduation from college. *Foreign Language Annals, 1,* 131-151.

Cazden, C.B. (1979). Curriculum/language contexts for bilingual education. In E.J. Briere (Ed.), *Language development in a bilingual setting* (pp. 129-138). Los Angeles, CA: National Dissemination and Assessment Center, California State University. (ERIC Document Reproduction Service No. ED 224 661)

Celce-Murcia, M., & Larsen-Freeman, D. (1983). *The grammar book.* Rowley, MA: Newbury House.

Chamot, A.U. (1983). Toward a functional ESL curriculum in the elementary school. *TESOL Quarterly, 17,* 459-471.

Chamot, A.U. (1985). English language development through a content-based approach. In *Issues in English language development.* Rosslyn, VA: National Clearinghouse for Bilingual Education.

Champagne, A. (1986). Children's ethno-science: An instructional perspective. In J.J. Gallagher & G.

Dawson (Eds.), *Science education & cultural environments in the Americas.* Washington, DC: National Science Teachers Association.

Cleland, C. (1981). Highlighting issues in children's literature through semantic webbing. *The Reading Teacher, 34,* 642-646.

Clement, J. (1981). *Algebra word problem solutions: Thought processes underlying a common misconception.* Unpublished manuscript. Amherst, MA: Department of Physics and Astronomy, Cognitive Development Project.

Cohen, E.G., & Anthony, B. (1982). *Expectation states theory and classroom learning.* Paper presented at the American Educational Research Association annual convention, New York.

Cohen, H.G. (1985). A comparison of the development of spatial conceptual abilities of students from two cultures. *Journal of Research in Science Teaching, 22,* 491-501.

Corle, C.G. (1974). Reading in mathematics: A review of recent research. In J.L. Laffey (Ed.), *Reading in the content areas.* Newark, DE: International Reading Association.

Cossio, M.G. (1978). The effects of language on mathematics placement scores in metropolitan colleges. *Dissertation Abstracts International, 38,* 4002A-4003A. (University Microfilms No. 77-27, 882).

Crandall, J.A., Dale, T.C., Rhodes, N., & Spanos, G. (1985, October). *The language of mathematics: The English barrier.* Paper presented at the Delaware Symposium on Language Studies VII. University of Delaware, Newark, DE.

Crandall, J.A., & Willetts, K. (1986). Content-based language instruction. *ERIC/CLL News Bulletin, 9*(2), 1, 7-8.

Cuevas, G.J. (1981, April). *SLAMS: A second language approach to mathematics learning.* Paper presented at the annual meeting of the National Council of Teachers of Mathematics, Toronto.

Cuevas, G.J. (1984). Mathematics learning in English as a second language. *Journal for Research in Mathematics Education, 15,* 134-144.

Cuevas, G.J., Mann, P., & McClung, R.M. (1985, April). *Language orientation to mathematics teaching.* Paper presented at the annual meeting of the American Psychological Association, Los Angeles.

Cummins, J. (1976). The influence of bilingualism on cognitive growth: A synthesis of research findings and explanatory hypotheses. *Working Papers on Bilingualism, 9,* 1-43.

Cummins, J. (1979). Linguistic interdependence and the educational development of bilingual children. *Review of Educational Research, 49,* 222-251.

Cummins, J. (1980). The construction of language proficiency in bilingual education. In J.E. Alatis (Ed.), *Current issues in bilingual education.* Washington, DC: Georgetown University Press.

Cummins, J. (1981). The role of primary language development in promoting educational success for language minority students. In *Schooling and language minority students: A theoretical framework.* Los Angeles: Evaluation, Dissemination and Assessment Center.

Cummins, J. (1982). *Tests, achievement and bicultural ambivalence.* Rosslyn, VA: National Clearinghouse for Bilingual Education.

Cummins, J. (1984). *Bilingualism and special education: Issues in assessment and pedagogy.* San Diego, CA: College-Hill.

Curtain, H.A. (1986). Integrating language and content instruction. *ERIC/CLL News Bulletin, 9*(2), 1, 10-11.

Dawe, L. (1983). Bilingualism and mathematical reasoning in English as a second language. *Educational Studies in Mathematics, 14,* 325-353.

Dawe, L. (1984). *A theoretical framework for the study of the effects of bilingualism on mathematics teaching and learning.* Paper presented at the Fifth International Congress on Mathematical Education, Adelaide, Australia.

De Avila, E. (1983). *Bilingualism, cognitive function and language minority group membership.* Unpublished manuscript. San Rafael, CA: Linguametrics Group.

De Avila, E., Cohen, E.G., & Intili, J.A. (1981). *Multicultural improvement of cognitive abilities: Final report.* Sacramento, CA: California State Department of Education.

De Avila, E., & Duncan, S. (1984). *Finding out and descubrimiento: Teacher's guide.* San Rafael, CA: Linguametrics Group.

Dolciani, M., & Wooten, W. (1970). *Modern alegebra: Structure and method* (Book 1) (rev. ed.). Boston: Houghton Mifflin.

Dupuis, N.M. (Ed.). (1984). *Reading in the content areas: Research for teachers.* Newark, DE: International Reading Association and ERIC Clearinghouse on Reading and Communication Skills.

Duran, R.P. (1980). *Bilinguals' skill in solving logical reasoning problems in two languages.* Unpublished manuscript. (ERIC Document Reproduction Service No. ED 198 724).

Erickson, F. (1986). Cultural difference and science education. In J.J. Gallagher & G. Dawson (Eds.), *Science education and cultural environments in the Americas.* Washington, DC: National Science Teachers Association.

Fathman, A., & Quinn, M.E. (forthcoming). *Science for language learners.* Oxford: Pergamon.

Fillmore, L.W. (1983). The language learner as an individual: Implications of research on individual differences for the ESL teacher. In M. Clarke & J. Handscombe (Eds.), *On TESOL '82: Pacific perspectives on language learning and teaching.* Washington, DC: Teachers of English to Speakers of Other Languages.

Fillmore, L.W. (1979). Individual differences in second language acquisition. In C. Fillmore, D. Kempler, & W. Wang (Eds.), *Individual differences in language ability and language behavior.* New York: Academic Press.

Firsching, J.T. (1982). Speaker expectations and mathematics word problems. *The SECOL Review, 3,* 35-47.

Freedman, G., & Reynolds, E. (1980). Enriching basal reader lessons with semantic webbing. *The Reading Teacher, 33,* 677-684.

Gardner, P.L. (1980). The identification of specific difficulties with logical connectives in science among secondary school students. *Journal of Research in Science Teaching, 17,* 223-229.

Garofalo, J., & Lester, F.K. (1985). Metacognition, cognitive monitoring, and mathematical performance. *Journal for Research in Mathematics Education, 16,* 163-176.

Hall, E.T. (1976). How cultures collide. *Psychology Today, 10,* 66-78.

Halliday, H.A.K. (1975). Some aspects of sociolinguistics. In E. Jacobsen (Ed.), *Interactions between linguistics and mathematical education: Final report of the symposium sponsored by UNESCO, CEDO and ICMI, Nairobi, Kenya, September 1-11, 1974* (UNESCO Report No. ED-74/ CONF.808, pp. 25-52). Paris: United Nations Educational, Scientific and Cultural Organization.

Hayes, C.W., & Bahruth, R. (1985). Querer es poder. In J. Hansen, T. Newkirk & D. Graves (Eds.), *Breaking ground: Teachers relate reading and writing in the elementary school.* Portsmouth, NH: Heinemann Educational Books.

Hayes, C.W., Bahruth, R., & Kessler, C. (1985, March). *To read you must write: Children in language acquisition.* Paper presented at the First International Conference on Second/Foreign Language Acquisition by Children, Oklahoma City, OK.

Hayes, M., & Pearce, A. (1985). *Northside elementary science curriculum—K.* San Antonio, TX: Northside School District.

Herber, H.L. (1978). *Teaching reading in the content areas* (2nd ed.). Englewood Cliffs, NJ: Prentice-Hall.

Ho, K.K. (1982). Effect of language of instruction on physics achievement. *Journal of Research in Science Teaching, 19,* 761-767.

Hurd, P.D., Robinson, J.T., McConnell, M.C., & Ross, N.M. (1981). *The status of middle and junior high school science.* Louisville, CO: Center for Educational Research and Evaluation, BSCS.

Johnson, D.M. (1983). Natural language learning by design: A classroom experiment in social interaction and second language acquisition. *TESOL Quarterly, 17,* 55-68.

Johnston, P. (1985). Writing to learn science. In A.R. Gere (Ed.), *Roots in the sawdust: Writing to learn across the disciplines.* Urbana, IL: National Council of Teachers of English.

Kessler, C., & Fathman, A. (1985). *ESL activities for HEATH SCIENCE, Levels 1-6.* Lexington, MA: D.C. Heath.

Kessler, C., & Quinn, M.E. (1980). Positive effects of bilingualism on science problem-solving abilities. In J.E. Alatis (Ed.), *Current issues in bilingual education: Proceedings from the Georgetown University Roundtable on Languages and Linguistics, 1980.* Washington, DC: Georgetown University Press.

Kessler, C., & Quinn, M.E. (1982). Cognitive development in bilingual environments. In B. Hartford, A. Valdman & C.R. Foster (Eds.), *Issues in international bilingual education.* New York: Plenum Press.

Kessler, C., & Quinn, M.E. (1984, April). *Second language acquisition in the context of science experiences.* Paper presented at the meeting of Teachers of English to Speakers of Other Languages, Houston, Tex. (ERIC Document Reproduction Service No. ED 248 713)

Kessler, C., & Quinn, M.E. (1985). Positive effects of bilingualism on science problem-solving abilities. In J.E. Alatis & J.J. Staczek (Eds.), *Perspectives on bilingualism and bilingual education.* Washington, DC: Georgetown University Press.

Kessler, C., Quinn, M.E., & Hayes, C.W. (1985, October). *Processing mathematics in a second language: Problems for LEP children.* Paper presented at the Delaware Symposium on Language Studies VII, University of Delaware, Newark, DE.

Knight, L., & Hargis, C. (1977). Math language ability: Its relationship to reading in math. *Language Arts, 54,* 423-428.

Krashen, S. (1981). *Second language acquisition and second language learning.* Oxford: Pergamon Press.

Krashen, S. (1982). *Principles and practice in second language acquisition.* Oxford: Pergamon Press.

Krashen, S. (1985). *Inquiries & insights.* Hayward, CA: Alemany Press.

Lambert, W., & Tucker, G.R. (1972). *Bilingual education of children.* Rowley, MA: Newbury House.

Lawson, A., Lawson, D.I., & Lawson, C.A. (1984). Proportional reasoning and the linguistic abilities required for hypothetico-deductive reasoning. *Journal of Research in Science Teaching, 21,* 119-131.

Lee, D., & Allen, R.V. (1963). *Learning to read through experience.* New York: Appleton-Century-Crofts.

Long, M.H., & Porter, P.A. (1985). Group work, interlanguage talk, and second language acquisition. *TESOL Quarterly, 19,* 207-228.

Lynch, P.P., Chipman, H.H., & Pachaury, A.C. (1985). The language of science and the high school student: The recognition of concept definitions: A comparison between Hindi speaking students in India and English speaking students in Australia. *Journal of Research in Science Teaching, 22,* 675-686.

Macnamara, J. (1966). *Bilingualism and primary education.* Edinburgh: Edinburgh University Press.

McCloskey, M. (1983). Intuitive physics. *Scientific American, 248*(4), 122-130.

McGroarty, M. (1985). *Teacher priorities in secondary ESL and EFL instruction.* Paper presented at CA-TESOL conference, San Diego, CA.

Mestre, J.P. (1984). The problem with problems: Hispanic students and math. *Bilingual Journal,* Fall, 15-20.

Mestre, J.P., Gerace, W.J., & Lockhead, J. (1982). The interdependence of language and translational math skills among bilingual Hispanic engineering students. *Journal of Research in Science Teaching, 19,* 399-410.

Milk, R. (1985). The changing role of ESL in bilingual education. *TESOL Quarterly, 18,* 657-672.

Mohan, B. (1979). Relating language teaching and content teaching. *TESOL Quarterly, 13*(2), 171-181.

Mohan, B.A. (1986a). *Language and content.* Reading, MA: Addison-Wesley.

Mohan, B.A. (1986b). Language and content learning: Finding common ground. *ERIC/CLL News Bulletin, 9*(2): 1, 8-9.

Morris, R.W. (1975). Linguistic problems encountered by contemporary curriculum projects in mathematics. In E. Jacobsen (Ed.), *Interactions between linguistics and mathematical education: Final report of the symposium sponsored by UNESCO, CEDO and ICMI, Nairobi, Kenya, September 1-11, 1974* (UNESCO Report No. Ed-74/CONF.808, p. 25-52). Paris: United Nations Educational, Scientific and Cultural Organization.

Mother nature's tiny wonders. (1984). R. Bahruth and fifth grade class, (Eds.) Pearsall, TX: Pearsall Independent School District.

Munro, J. (1979). Language abilities and maths performance. *Reading Teacher, 32*(2), 900-915.

Oller, J.W., Baca, L.L., & Vigil, A. (1978). Attitudes and attained proficiency in ESL: A sociolinguistic study of Mexican-Americans in the Southwest. *TESOL*

Quarterly, 11, 173-183.

Penfield, J., & Ornstein-Galicia, J. (1981). Language through science: An integrative model. In R.V. Padilla (Ed.), *Ethnoperspectives in bilingual education research.* Ypsilanti, MI: Eastern Michigan University Press.

Piaget, J. (1926). *The language and thought of the child.* New York: Harcourt, Brace.

Quinn, M.E., & Kessler, C. (1984, December). *Bilingual children's cognition and language in science learning.* Paper presented at the Inter-American Seminar on Science Education, Panama.

Quinn, M.E., & Kessler, C. (1986). Bilingual children's cognition and language in science learning. In J.J. Gallagher & G. Dawson (Eds.), *Science education & cultural environments in the Americas,* Washington, DC: National Science Teachers Association.

Reutzel, D.R. (1985). Story maps improve comprehension. *The Reading Teacher, 38,* 400-404.

Robinson, F.P. (1962). *Effective reading.* New York: Harper and Row.

Rodriguez, I., & Bethel, L.J. (1983). An inquiry approach to science and language teaching. *Journal of Research in Science Teaching, 20,* 291-296.

Saville-Troike, M. (1984). What really matters in second language learning for academic achievement. *TESOL Quarterly, 18,* 199-219.

Sinatra, R., & Stahl-Gemake, J. (1983). *Using the right brain in the language arts.* Springfield, IL: Charles C Thomas.

Smith, F. (1975). *Comprehension and learning: A conceptual framework for teachers.* New York: Holt, Rinehart & Winston.

Smith, M. (1986). A model for teaching native oriented science. In J.J. Gallagher & G. Dawson (Eds.), *Science education & cultural environments in the Americas.* Washington, DC: National Science Teachers Association.

Spiegel, D.L. (1981). Six alternatives to the directed reading activity. *The Reading Teacher, 34,* 914-920.

Suydam, M.N. (1982). Update on research on problem solving: Implications for classroom teaching. *Arithmetic Teacher, 29*(6), 56-60.

Swain, M. (1984). A review of immersion education in Canada: Research and evaluation studies. In *Studies on immersion: A collection for United States educators.* Sacramento, CA: California Dept. of Education, Office of Bilingual Bicultural Education.

Swales, J. (1985). *Episodes in ESP.* Oxford, U.K.: Pergamon.

Tchudi, S.N., & Herta, M.C. (1983). *Teaching writing in the content areas: Middle school/junior high.* Washington, DC: National Education Association.

Tchudi, S.N., & Tchudi, S.J. (1983). *Teaching writing in the content areas: Elementary school.* Washington, DC: National Education Association.

Tchudi, S.N., & Yates, J. (1983). *Teaching writing in the content areas: Senior high school.* Washington, DC: National Education Association.

Titone, R. (1981). The holistic approach to second language education. In *The Second Language Classroom.* New York: Oxford University Press.

Tritch, D. (1984). *Logical connectors and scientific register.* Unpublished manuscript. The University of Texas at San Antonio.

Vacca, R.T. (1981). *Content area reading.* Boston: Little Brown.

Ventriglia, L. (1982). *Conversations of Miguel and Maria.* Reading, MA: Addison-Wesley.

Wayman, J.G. (1985). Reaching and teaching the gifted child. *Challenge, 4*(1), 2-4.

Wilson, B.E.A., De Avila, E., & Intili, J.K. (1982, April). *Improving cognitive, linguistic and academic skills in bilingual classrooms.* Paper presented at the annual meeting of the American Educational Research Association, New York.

Yager, R.E. (1983). The importance of teaching terminology in K-12 science. *Journal of Research in Science Teaching, 20,* 577-588.